Political Alienation
in Contemporary America

Robert S. Gilmour
Robert B. Lamb

St. Martin's Press   New York

To our children—
Robert, Jr., James, Kara, Corinna, and Robert

Preface

During the fall of 1972, part-time student and full-time union man Carmello Charles Gallo set about to verify statistically his belief that blue-collar workers had become the most politically dissatisfied people in America. The authors shared Gallo's hunch about the alienated worker, but we also supposed that the disease of political alienation had spread well beyond the blue-collar strata into economic and social realms where the voices of deep political estrangement had seldom been heard before. With Charles Gallo's invaluable assistance, we decided to expand the investigation to include a much larger cross-section of American society.

For all the commentary, interviews, discussions, and books on the American character and public opinion, almost nothing of substance has been done to clarify and measure the complex of feelings we have called political alienation or to assess its importance for the American future. That is the reason for this book—to sort out these feelings, to comprehend their extent and change, to locate their sources and probable effects. Our aim has been to develop a measurement of political alienation that is firmly grounded in the best and most consistent samples of American opinion, and through personal interviews with the people who have come to feel this sense of disillusion and distance, to present their responses to American politics over more than a decade.

We are deeply grateful to the many people who supported our ideas and assisted our efforts in writing this book.

More than two hundred people took the time to tell their stories and share their views on American politics. In many ways, theirs is the message and meaning of this book.

The Interuniversity Consortium for Political Research at the University of Michigan made available survey data from the national presidential election studies conducted by Angus Campbell, Philip Converse, Warren Miller, and Donald Stokes. Stephen Butts and Pnina Grinberg of Columbia University's Bureau of Applied Social Research and Professor Gerald Finch helped secure and reformat these data for use in New York.

Douglas M. Fox, Fred Grupp, Richard Ned Lebow, and Richard Pious carefully read the entire manuscript, providing both generous encouragement and unreluctant criticism.

Nancy Axelrod, Judith Brown, Joseph DeBonis, Ennis Duling, Dell Feuerlicht, Kay Avery Feuerlicht, Dall Forseyth, Martha Heitkamp, Peter Heitkamp, Rick Kenney, William Lamb, Corliss Lamont, Harold Laswell, Rachael O'Mara, Margaret Reich, Sally Sady, Derek Wittner, David Wright, and Richard Wright offered helpful comments on all or part of the manuscript. Geoffrey Ginos, Susan Ogulnick, and Edward Volchok took part in the initial research and bibliographic work.

The reference and research librarians at Middlebury College Library, Castleton State College Library, University of Vermont Library, and Columbia University Libraries unfailingly gave us their generous assistance, as did the research consultants at Columbia University Computer Center.

We are especially grateful to Nanette Gilmour, who lent a critical editorial eye to every draft, typed the final one, and generally helped to make the writing an enjoyable task.

ROBERT S. GILMOUR
ROBERT B. LAMB

Contents

Political Alienation
in Contemporary America

chapter 1

Political Disillusion and Alienation

JENNY IS HANGING out her family's wash on the pulley line that stretches from her tenement window. The welfare caseworker is still there after half an hour, and Jenny is again explaining how she "just can't make the food stamps go far 'nough with all these prices risin' up so." Jenny glances around the dismal room, fearing that the woman has spotted her boyfriend's boots by the big chair or maybe his underwear in the wash-basket or something else that might stop the welfare checks. Later she tells us, "Seems like all they want is to get somethin' on me. Here they makin' big money an' comin' 'round checkin' on me, an' I ain't got nothin'. Ain' nobody up there in Wash'-ton cares 'bout folks like me or my chil'ren. I use' ta think they was gonna do somethin', but no more. Now all they want is ta tell *us* what ta do. An' they ain' nothin' we can do."

Ralph is a forty-four-year-old truck driver. He's more than a thousand miles away from home in a truck-stop diner, being force-fed a political campaign speech over the TV while he finishes his hash browns. Annoyed, he watches in spite of himself. He scans the other eyes down the counter. It's then he realizes he's shaking his head back and forth, and so is the old man on the stool at the end of the counter. So is the

1

waitress. One of the men breathes a curse. "Aw, why doncha turn it off," Ralph says out loud. "They're all the same." "Yeah," the old man at the end agrees, "ain't none of 'em worth two cents."

Over her coffee at her community college snack bar, Sharon speaks intensely about the President. "He makes me wanna vomit! Would you believe my history professor is trying to give us a big rap on why we should register and vote? He's gotta be kidding! What possible difference could it make? Ford and Rockefeller are almost as bad as Nixon! . . . They're all so corrupt, and there just isn't anything you can do about it. Washington politics is just so big, so far out there, I just can't relate. I don't even read about it anymore."

Alan is nearing retirement in San Diego, California. He looks up at his bookkeeper from his accounting ledgers: "God, I can't wait till I can stop looking into everybody else's problems with the government and just retire. This damn government causes a hell of a lot more trouble than it's ever solved." The young assistant mumbles, "Yeah," while continuing to push the figures, not really listening to this much repeated refrain. "Now those bastards want us to pay the Russians three times as much for grain as we sold it to them for last year. Hell, it didn't even leave the country. And half those birds now have cushy jobs with the grain companies for lining up the deal. For this I should pay damn near half my income in taxes!"

These are just a few of the voices of disillusionment, political alienation, and apathy. Each is different; each has an individual point of view, but each represents some aspect of that growing sector in America that no longer believes the words of politicians, distrusts their actions, motives, salaries, and income tax statements. These are the Americans who are convinced of the essential meaninglessness of votes, candidates, parties, and elections. They conceive of themselves as the victims of powerful forces in politics that are beyond understanding and control.

The American involvement in the Vietnam war, the increasing invasions of bureaucracy at all levels into our private lives, the political intrigues, trickery, and outright criminality of the nation's highest officials—all these have pushed many people to the very edge of allegiance to the political system they once cherished.

Political Alienation

Despite vague and contradictory meanings of "political alienation," there is broad agreement that alienation does indeed exist. Informed but less optimistic observers, such as Louis Harris, claim that the proportion of Americans who are alienated from their national government is 50 percent and higher. The evidence for such a judgment is all but overwhelming from the newspaper, magazine, TV reports; opinion polls; and surveys we reviewed and analyzed. But it was the extended personal interviews we held with a variety of people that brought the point most forcefully and convincingly home.

The characteristic comment was made by a retired fireman: "Watergate has convinced me that what I thought happened sometimes happens *all* the time." A similar view was stated by a Denver druggist: "Perhaps I felt this way even without Watergate. My taxes go up after every election, while politicians take their junkets to Europe, get contracts for their friends and kickbacks on roads and other projects. They always seem to have their hands in the till. It sure beats working for a living."

The widespread sense of *distrust* resulting from the Watergate scandals, the numerous indictments and convictions, and the investigation and subsequent resignations of Vice President Spiro Agnew and President Richard Nixon should not be allowed to obscure the view of other, almost equally wide-

3

spread aspects of disillusionment and political alienation that have now become well rooted in the public mind. A sense of the *meaninglessness* of choice between poor candidates and outmoded parties was echoed wherever we went. "It doesn't matter which way you vote; they're all the same, talk the same, promise the same. But all out for themselves, that's all," was a Boston doorman's way of summing up this meaninglessness of choice.

A sense of *powerlessness* to make any political impact or to make needed changes of direction was another repeated theme. "I am powerless to influence any political vote, any political decision, or any politician," a New Jersey housewife explained. "There's no relation between my vote and what any politician does," a New York City cabdriver said. "It's like worshipping a pagan god, 'cause once you vote for them they never again have any contact with you." A heavy-equipment operator in Iowa summed up all these feelings. When asked about representative government, he shot back, "What representation of the people? They don't even know who the people are. The Democrats and Republicans are just the same. They only represent one thing: Number One, and maybe a crony or two." While he rolled silently across a crowded golf course in his electric cart, a Chicago investor remarked, "We used to joke about politics in '1984' but now it's hitting you in the face, and it's frightening."

In spite of the keen sense of distance, disdain, and even fear felt by the governed for their governors, many of our informants agreed with the widow of a TV repairman in Memphis: "We don't need to change the Constitution. Not one bit. The problem is what they're doing with it. They're twisting it all out of shape." The people we interviewed consistently saw a basic difference between "the constitution" or "the government" and elected officials: "Kick them out and start over again!" a summer stock stagehand demanded. "Why?" we asked. "I can't trust any of them. It's just a feeling I have. I

4

don't care if it's a judge or the President or the parking meter guy. Everybody knows they're crooks." "Vote out everybody in office, is what I say," an upstate New York mason said. Others saw the distinction between government structure and the politicians clearly enough, but they were less optimistic about the effectiveness of an electoral clean sweep. "I guess they all gits crooked when they gits that high up," the wife of an elderly New England potato farmer said. "Guess they has to be." An estranged student put an ideological cast on the same theme: "They're all just in there tight with the big capitalists and the big bucks. The whole system's set up that way now. What's my vote gonna mean to that? Nothing!"

In this book we define political disillusionment and alienation as the combination of several distinct feelings: *distrust* of government and politicians, a sense of the *meaninglessness* of electoral politics and political choices, and personal *powerlessness* to influence or change the course of American political life. Disillusionment with government might begin with any one of these feelings, but thoroughgoing alienation—the end of faith in the practice of American politics—we contend, is a combination of all three.

We have drawn our definition of alienation from the conceptions of theorists and social thinkers, ranging from Jean Jacques Rousseau, Adam Smith, and Karl Marx, from Christian religious philosophers, and from the writings of contemporary political sociologists. The thoughts of each have differed in emphasis and detail, but there is a substantial similarity.

The intent of our study, however, is to measure the depth of these feelings across a broad spectrum of the American public over many years' time. We want to see with some certainty who the politically disillusioned and alienated people are in America and which people are coming to feel this way, whether they are urban ghetto dwellers, laborers, young professionals, farmers, or what have you. It is then possible to

5

find out how these people take part in, or drop out of, present-day politics, and what roles they may play in the politics of the future. It can be shown that the numbers of alienated Americans are increasing substantially and that their part in shaping the future may be crucial. But the place to begin is with the development of the idea of *political alienation* as distinct from simple disillusionment or political apathy.

The Idea of Alienation

The notion of alienation originated in early Christian thought. For centuries, the feeling of being at one with God was contrasted with the feeling of being separated or alien from God. In the Middle Ages, the term had three additional connotations: first, it had the meaning of transferring ownership; second, it was used to describe mental disorders; and third, it meant interpersonal estrangement, that is, to make warm relations between people cool or to make oneself disliked.[1]

Rousseau and Smith. The broader economic and social implications of alienation were first elaborated by Jean Jacques Rousseau's theory of the corruption of natural man. Rousseau, a young student living in mid-eighteenth-century Paris envisioned man living in the state of nature. From this state of goodness, he said, man has steadily become twisted, distorted, and dehumanized by society and government. In his famous *Discourse on the Origin of Inequality,* Rousseau painted a disturbing portrait of man's corruption through social controls, customs, needs, drives, passions, institutions, practices, and habits.[2]

This argument was originally interpreted by his literary friends and rivals as a humorous twist on the conventional idea that civilization had improved man. They thought he was making a joke about civilization, because they knew it had lifted men from a life of starvation, of scraping the

6

barren hillsides and marshes, and foraging game and berries. Civilization had brought the sublime ease, culture, genteel manners, and sophisticated conversation that were greatly admired. But Rousseau's portrait was hardly meant to amuse. His description of an alienated society was not only a critique of the wasteful gossip and outmoded manners of the gentry and nobility; it was a direct thrust at the diseases of commercial life and the resulting corruption of the arts, sciences, laws, and humanity itself.

Rousseau stated that once the institution of private property was established in society, great inequality developed and the alienated individuals who composed society stood exposed as "an assemblage of artificial men with factitious passions which are the work of all these new relations and have no true foundation in nature." [3] For Rousseau, human alienation meant specifically that civilization had removed or estranged man from his natural condition. By associating with the social system, man has transmitted all of his rights to the community.[4] He has lost his natural passions and abilities and replaced them with distorted, complicated modern social arrangements. The noble savage is no more; "Man is born free; and everywhere he is in chains." [5]

Rousseau did not want man to return to nature, and, in fact, he did *not* believe man capable of returning to his "natural" condition. Yet Rousseau did catalogue the numerous losses of human capabilities that men have sustained by their transformation during centuries of civilization and their subsequent "detachment" from society.[6]

Adam Smith, the Scottish professor who founded modern economics, expanded Rousseau's theme of social alienation.[7] Smith went into far greater detail in his analysis of industrial societies. He concluded that the factory worker, trapped in a single narrow task for months or years, "becomes as stupid and ignorant as it is possible for a human creature to become." [8] In Smith's view, the uniformity of the worker's sta-

Political Alienation

tionary life naturally corrupts the courage of his mind and the
activity of his body, rendering him incapable of exerting his
strength with vigor and perserverance to different employment. Of the extent of this alienation of workers, Smith stated,
"In every improved and civilized society, this is the state into
which the labouring poor, that is, the great body of the people,
must necessarily fall, unless government takes some pains to
prevent it." [9]

As industrialism and commercialism continued to develop,
it followed from Smith's argument that human self-estrangement would vastly increase. Smith mentioned the three kinds
of human alienation that Hegel and Marx were to make
famous. He demonstrated various ways in which factory life,
long hours, and narrow, specialized trades were making men
powerless, isolated, and "mutilated and deformed in a still
more essential part of the character of human nature." [10]

Hegel and Marx.   It is not generally realized that the re-
nowned German philosopher Friedrich Hegel based much of
his concept of alienation on the thinking of Rousseau and
Smith. For Hegel, the alienation of man resulted from private
ownership. He argued that laws, customs, and institutions all
prevent the real satisfaction of human needs. The more that
modern work is transferred to machines or mechanized processes, the less men develop their separate creative capacities,
and thus they become increasingly alienated. But once men
realize that their alienation prevents them from creatively developing, then it ceases to be a confining wall. Instead, it becomes a hurdle to leap over and a part of their training in
self-awareness. Without objects, tasks, and problems to overcome, no self-consciousness can develop.

Hegel argued that to achieve self-consciousness, men and
states must proceed through a constant antagonism of one
force against another, one idea against another—a dialectic.
Each thesis generates its own contradictory antithesis, and out

8

of the struggle between these two alien forces comes a new synthesis. Thus the process of alienation is not static but is constantly changing and can be continually analyzed on either a philosophic level or on the concrete level of historic social changes.[11]

Hegel's greatest disciple in the study of alienation was Karl Marx, and it is Marx's sense of the term that is still generally in use. For Marx, alienation meant the separation of man from his humanness and from his natural social development. The causes of alienation are found in the economic, political, and social facts of capitalist industrial life. These facts, however, can be discovered and changed; man need not always be alienated. Although certain major points about alienation are presented in *Das Kapital,* the main theory of alienation is expressed in Marx's *Economic and Philosophic Manuscripts of 1844,* written while he was a student, and not discovered or published until 1926. Marx describes three critical aspects of alienation: powerlessness, isolation, and self-estrangement. By these he meant that men are estranged from the process of work, the objects they make, and from their species being.[12]

According to Marx, the worker is powerless in the capitalist system and capitalist society, in contracts with his employer, and in the amount and manner in which he is paid. The hours he works, the conditions of hardship, the tools he uses, and the products he makes are all determined by the capitalist who employs him and to whom he must submit for daily subsistence. Marx further argues that the worker is isolated in his narrow tasks; he no longer works on complete products but only produces a small part. Thus he has become ignorant of the entire process of work and the nature of the product he makes. Long hours and unrewarding tasks keep him apart from his friends and family. He feels at home with himself only when he is not working. As a result, his labor is forced, and work is an alien activity. Finally, this process of isolation from his work and from fellow humans estranges each man

9

from his own humanity. Marx says, "The worker becomes all the poorer the more wealth he produces. . . . The worker becomes an even cheaper commodity the more commodities he creates. . . . The increasing value of the world of things proceeds in direct proportion to the devaluation of men." [13] And the worse off he makes himself vis-à-vis the capitalist who steadily builds up more capital for further exploitation.

Like Adam Smith, Marx saw alienation as a steadily increasing and worsening phenomenon. And like Hegel, Marx considered this steady destruction of men as ultimately beneficial, because it is only through men's becoming conscious of their own alienation that they can gradually come to develop self-consciousness. Only then can they understand their social exploitation. Alienation is therefore necessary for social revolution. However painful and intense it becomes, it is the disease that can cure human and social ills.

Marx's primary link to modern theories of political alienation is his concept that the state apparatus, and power, is always alien to the vast majority of the people because it is the instrument of the ruling class for the continued suppression of all others. "Political power, properly so-called, is merely the organized power of one class for oppressing another." [14]

After Marx. The anarchists, Nihilists, populists, and utopians to some extent helped develop the concept of alienation by their mere existence and activities, by attacking society or building sanctuaries from the human soul-destructiveness of cities or states. Their declarations of discontent, whether they resulted in the assassination of a czar, in the establishment of a commune in Oneida, New York, or on the barren sands of Palestine, in the ringing declarations of political campaigns, or in the writing of gentle philosophic pamphlets, continued to focus attention on the political alienation of various parts of society throughout the nineteenth century and beyond.[15]

In the twentieth century, social scientists have developed

extensive theories of alienation that often use Marxian thought as a point of departure for their detailed elaborations of minor constructs or for pointed examinations of work alienation in factories and offices or of other forms of social estrangement.[16] Others have focused quite directly on the political content of alienation in modern society, distinguishing politics from economics and social structure in a way that Marx would not have allowed.[17] A number of these studies are noted for reference, but for our purposes here, the most useful contemporary work is that of political scientist Ada Finifter.[18]

Using the tools of advanced statistics and the computer, Finifter has uncovered relationships among a variety of political and social attitudes expressed by Americans in a sample survey. In Finifter's study, political alienation is understood as clusters or "dimensions" of statistically different kinds of alienation, which bear a striking resemblance to the definitions developed by Adam Smith and Karl Marx.[19] More importantly, Finifter's work suggests a method based on public opinion sampling rather than speculation as the means to define the concept.[20]

Measuring the Depths

It is one thing to have a sound and thoughtful definition of political alienation; it is quite another to measure the depth and scope of these feelings, to find their location in society, and to gauge their importance with any assurance.[21] Here is where the statistically based techniques of the sample survey and the attitude scale offer considerable assistance. They are at once powerful in sorting out a large number and variety of opinions or other information and relatively simple to use and understand.

The major sources for the percentages and tabulations presented here are the national election surveys of public opinion conducted by the University of Michigan's Institute for Social

Research (ISR). These samples of about 2,000 to 2,500 people across the country have been repeated during every presidential election campaign since 1952, and they are generally regarded as the most reliable sources for the study of American political opinion. Since many of the survey questions dealing with cynicism, estrangement, and disinterest were repeated during every survey since 1960, it is possible to build attitude scales to measure those attitudes with some accuracy over several presidential elections.

The ISR election surveys have a distinguished tradition of accuracy and scholarly detachment, but no sample survey is a perfect barometer of mass opinion. Sampling variations are statistically bound to occur, and crises, news events, or hidden prejudices may prompt peculiar responses to certain questions at any given moment. What is even more troubling, especially to the potential respondent or general critic of survey research, is that no survey question is precisely fitted to the attitude or statement of fact he wants expressed. And no set of answers has exactly the response he feels is right. On hearing the questions, he is forced to offer answers that weren't quite what he had in mind. And further explanations aren't normally allowed, because they aren't intelligible to the computer, however meaningful they may be to us. Still, it is usually possible to choose the answer that "most nearly" expresses feelings about a problem, an idea, or a political candidate. This makes possible the tabulation of at least general trends in the way different groups of people feel about things political. The point here is that these tabulations cannot precisely reflect the national mood, but if the sample is carefully drawn, the overall tendencies they reflect are not likely to be misleading.

The condition of a "carefully drawn" sample cannot be stressed enough, since a biased sample inevitably leads to unwarranted and sometimes disastrously wrong conclusions. The *Literary Digest* election survey of 1936 is something of a legend in this regard. Shortly before the election, the *Digest* showed Governor Alf Landon of Kansas defeating President

Franklin D. Roosevelt by a large margin; in fact, Roosevelt won the election with the largest presidential majority in history.[22] In conducting their "scientific" survey, the editor-surveyors selected respondents from lists of city and suburban telephone subscribers in a depression year when most voters were either unemployed or couldn't afford a monthly phone bill. These phone books identified the very core of 1936 Republicanism, and the *Digest* never recovered from its error.

Because of ISR's wide-ranging survey experience and rigorous techniques, our work with the national election surveys is more solidly based than that of the ill-fated *Literary Digest*. But excellent as these statistics may be and however carefully we may make our tabulations, a most crucial fact remains: we are dealing with real people who have their own special views of government and politics.

Distrust. Jack is helping a neighbor fix a decrepit Vermont barn. The men move at a slow but steady pace. Jack reminisces warmly about the old days when they "farmed it" with horses "over to Tinmouth" and when "fifteen cows made a decent living for a man and his family." When talk meanders over to politics, Jack's memories turn to scorn: "Why they raisin' the' selves up thousands, an' us up pennies. An' we're spose' to make a go of it on $176 a month with prices raisin' up all to hell! They use' to say that the Republicans was the rich people an' the Democrats was the poor people. Now the Democrats is crooked, and the Republicans is even more crooked!"

Not everyone feels distrustful of government in quite the way Jack does, but all respondents in the national surveys were asked quite pointedly about their trust in government, the honesty of its leaders, and about the performance of public officials as representatives of the people. The most distrustful responses were as follows*:

* The exact questions asked and the variety of responses offered to respondents in the national surveys are found in the appendix.

> I think that quite a few people running the government, maybe all of them, are a little crooked.

> It's very rare that we can trust the government in Washington to do the right thing.

> I would say that the government is pretty much run by a few big interests looking out for themselves and not for the benefit of all people.

The general feeling is that the government is no longer "of the people, by the people, and for the people." Instead, the government is in the hands of corrupt officials in Washington whose job it is to watch out primarily for the vested interests of an elite sector of society.

These responses were generated by questions that were used to form a definite scale of distrust in government. The questions chosen best approximated the powerful scale of attitude measurement defined by Louis Guttman some twenty-five years ago.[23] The Guttman Scale is made up of questions that are highly interrelated. A person who answers with a distrustful response on one question is very likely to answer the same way on one of the others. The scale is also cumulative. The questions have a definite rank order showing different degrees of distrust. For example, when the three distrust questions were asked, fewer people answered "that the government is pretty much run by a few big interests" than gave distrusting answers to the other two questions. But those who did give the "run by a few big interests" response were likely to say that they couldn't "trust the government . . . to do the right thing" and that many or all government officials were "a little crooked." And so it goes in rank order with the second and third questions. Taken as a group of three indicators, these questions measure the degree of political distrust.[24]

Powerlessness. "You kiddin' me, man?" Larry blazed at us near his home in Bunche Park, Florida. "Black people don' have no power in government. Those politicians don' do nothin' for me. Nothin'! Don' nobody doesn' have a million dollars gets any help, man, even if they's white. . . . You think votin' in a black man in a city that's mostly black—that's black power? Man, that dude's gonna do what the white man say an' what they give him money to do."

Not only angry young blacks like Larry feel outraged at their political impotence; many of the elderly, women, and even successful professionals have begun to feel the same way. In the national election studies, the survey question responses that best reflected these feelings were:

> People like me don't have much say at all about what the government does.

> Politics and government are so complicated that people like me can't really understand what's going on.

> Most public officials don't care much at all about what people like me think.

The three questions that identified this sense of citizen power-lessness to influence or understand the government also approximated a Guttman Scale.

Meaninglessness. "I just don't think the political parties mean much anymore," Carol said in her suburban, Ann Arbor living room. "I mean, really, they're just the same; at least I can't tell any difference. Why, Nixon seemed pretty bad, but just think about Ted Kennedy. He's got his Chappaquiddick, doesn't he? And didn't he get caught cheating or something? I don't see why we even have parties anymore. What we really need are some good men in government, not these party hacks."

Political meaninglessness means that the individual voter believes the political choices offered him are irrelevant, that they are, in actuality, nonchoices. It makes no difference which party is in power; one party is just as inconsequential

15

to the individual's goals and well-being as the other. The voter feels that he has no genuine choice in the decision-making process, and that the result of his vote and that of many others will have no effect after election day has passed. Alienated citizens' responses to the several questions on political meaning were as follows:

> It won't make any difference whether the Democrats or the Republicans are elected in terms of getting what I want done about (the most important national problem singled out by the citizen answering).

> It won't make any difference whether the Democrats or the Republicans are elected in terms of getting what I want done about (the second most important national problem identified by the respondent).

> It won't make any difference in how my family and I get along financially whether the Republicans or the Democrats win the election.

The first things we learned by examining responses in the three scales were that distrust, powerlessness, and meaninglessness are distinct and increasingly widespread feelings among the electorate. Expressed in a statistical way, these are three "discrete dimensions" of political alienation, each of them increasing at a slightly different rate. The upward sweep in the percentages of political distrust, powerlessness, and meaninglessness felt by Americans during the 1960–1972 period is shown in Figure 1-1. The variety of feelings expressed might better be illustrated by many black Americans who have consistently believed that there was an important distinction to be made between the two major political parties. This isn't surprising, since in recent years blacks have been overwhelmingly attracted to the Democratic Party.[25] At the same time, many blacks have expressed the sense of political powerlessness and distrust felt by Larry in Bunche Park when he said that "no politician" would ever do "nothin' " for him.

16

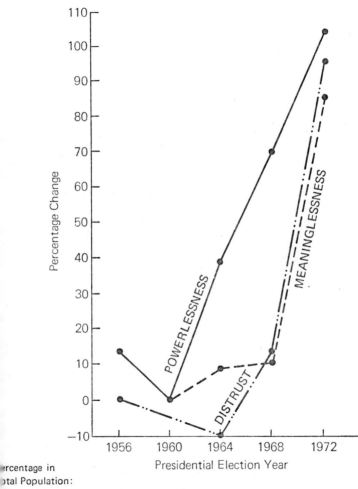

Percentage Change in American Feelings of Political
Distrust,[a] Powerlessness, and Meaninglessness,[b] 1956-1972[c]

Percentage in
Total Population:

	1956	1960	1964	1968	1972
DISTRUST	12.8		11.5	14.6	25.0
POWERLESSNESS	15.5	13.7	19.0	23.3	28.0
MEANINGLESSNESS		28.1	30.2	30.8	52.0

FIGURE 1-1.
Percentage Change in American Feelings of Political
Distrust,[a] Powerlessness, and Meaninglessness,[b] 1956-1972[c]

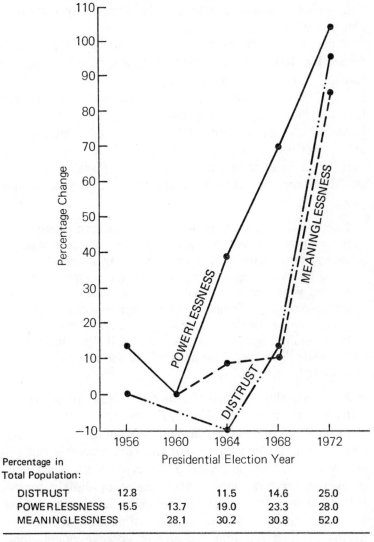

Percentage in Total Population:					
DISTRUST	12.8		11.5	14.6	25.0
POWERLESSNESS	15.5	13.7	19.0	23.3	28.0
MEANINGLESSNESS		28.1	30.2	30.8	52.0

[a]Questions on political *distrust* were asked of the 1956 ISR panel, but they were not repeated in 1960.

[b]Only one of the three political *meaninglessness* questions was asked in the ISR survey in 1972.

[c]1960 is set as the base year in calculating percentage change.

When Larry was asked if there was a difference between the two parties, he responded, "Every black person knows what the Republicans is and who they is. That's why they votes Democrat!"

Differences in political disillusionment appear in several forms. Dr. Joseph L., for instance, is a successful dentist in southern Illinois. "I can't honestly say that I feel powerless," he said. "I've built up a decent practice, and even with this fantastic inflation, I've been able to keep up pretty well. I know a lot of the people in local office, and I imagine I'm able to get my ideas across about as well as anyone." However, when he considers the honesty of national leaders and the importance of national parties, Dr. L. has quite another point of view:

> I don't feel . . . well, when I hear my children saying
> parties, promises, and elections don't matter anymore, that
> it doesn't matter which party gets elected any longer, I'm
> afraid I've had to agree with them. That doesn't mean I've
> stopped voting; of course not. But the out-and-out
> corruption, the deceit, and the phony posturing of politicians
> in both parties have me very, very discouraged. Now even
> President Ford seems to have been in on this Nixon mess.
> I honestly don't know how much of this the country
> can stand.

A considerable number of Americans who are succeeding in their work or business have not come to feel that government has become too complicated for them to "really understand" what is going on or that the government is run primarily for the "big interests." Yet they do feel a keen sense of distrust for politicians and disinterest or disdain for the political choices offered them in the polling booths. Still others, a smaller number, believe that most political leaders are worthy of trust but that the growth of government, lookalike political parties, and an electoral system based on the deceit of TV imagery have let them down and diminished their importance as citizens.

The three dimensions of political estrangement we have measured are clearly not one and the same but they are interrelated. It is possible, therefore, to create a combined index of political alienation using all nine questions. To say that a person is "politically alienated," for example, may mean that he feels extremely distrustful of government and powerless to change its course, but that he feels somewhat less strongly that party differences are meaningless. While such differences of feeling exist, it is often useful to ignore them in favor of a larger overview. For our purposes here, we refer to the "extremely alienated" Americans as those persons who answered at least seven of our nine question indicators in ways that express their political disillusion and estrangement.* Thus, it can be seen in Figure 1-2 that the overall pattern of change in citizen feelings is one of markedly increasing estrangement between 1960 and 1972. Understandably, this pattern is largely the same as those already shown.

In 1960, extreme political alienation during the presidential contest between John F. Kennedy and Richard Nixon was quite low. Americans were relatively affluent, and both candidates expressed youthful confidence for a hopeful and vigorous national future. In 1964, at a time when the death of President Kennedy weighed heavily on the minds of many Americans, the intense national contest between the conservative backers of Barry Goldwater and "Great Society" liberal supporters of President Lyndon Johnson generated widespread feeling that the political outcome was important.[26] Extreme political alienation declined slightly, as a sense of political urgency increased. Since 1964, however, the number of extremely alienated citizens has been steadily on the increase. Widespread political disillusionment, or partial alienation on the combined index, has remained relatively constant, and firm political allegiance has declined.

Political alienation reached a measurable peak in 1972, dur-

* A more technical discussion of the combination index of political alienation is found in the appendix on methods at the end of the book.

19

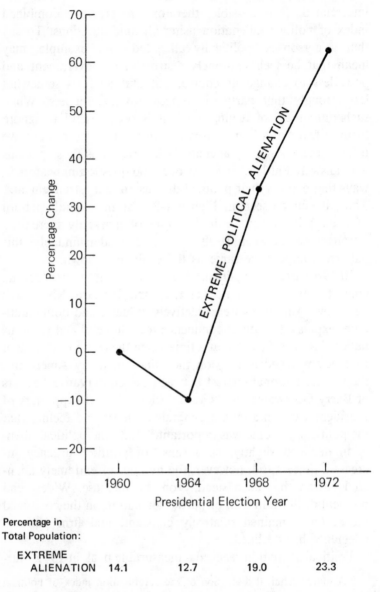

FIGURE 1-2.
Percentage Change in American Feelings of Extreme
Political Alienation, 1960-1972[a]

Percentage in
Total Population:

	1960	1964	1968	1972
EXTREME ALIENATION	14.1	12.7	19.0	23.3

[a]1960 is set as the base year in calculating percentage change.

ing the presidential contest between President Nixon and Senator George McGovern, even though their contrasting philosophies were well known to most voters. But the scandal of Watergate was already breaking and, the unseemly selection and rejection of Democratic vice-presidential candidate Tom Eagleton had received front-page and prime-time coverage. Informal indicators and national polls since the 1972 campaign suggest that the swelling tide of alienation continues to increase at an alarming rate. The revelations of Watergate and the indictments, convictions, and resignations at the highest levels of government have no doubt played their part in the rising distrust, cynicism, and disgust of the citizens for their governors and for their very system of government.

Many commentators believe that political alienation leads logically to apathy and withdrawal from politics, and a few have used the two ideas as synonyms. We find, however, that most alienated citizens are still interested and active in national politics. As we shall see in Chapter 5, *political apathy* is a different idea entirely. The apathetic citizen is uninterested and inattentive to politics and usually withdraws from active involvement.

Now that we have a tool to identify America's alienated citizens, our first task is to learn more exactly who they are and to attempt to find out how they have come to feel the way they do. In Chapter 6, this index will again be used to discover the political thoughts of alienated Americans and how they are likely to take political action. Finally, the question must be raised: What importance does the vast increase in political alienation hold for the American political future?

chapter 2

The Alienated Americans

Jenny Jackson

In 1960, the most typical alienated person in America might have been Jenny Jackson. Jenny, who was twenty and black, lived on a sharecropping farm with her parents in rural Arkansas. Jenny's parents and grandparents had always lived in the area and never looked to government for anything but trouble. No one in the family had ever voted. Their annual income was barely above the income tax filing level, and yet they couldn't qualify for government subsidies or services. Politics, whether local or national, was an alien white force that put "Whites Only" signs on water fountains, toilets, and luncheonettes. Segregation was still very much alive. Despite the 1954 Supreme Court desegregation decision in *Brown* v. *The Board of Education,* the local school still had only black students and black teachers.[1] Only the white children went to the new school in the valley. Jenny's three teachers shied away from any mention of politics, and what political conversation she had overheard at home was vague and minimal. Gossip and rumor made her suspect that politics might be connected with the whites who ran the Ku Klux Klan—those same whites who were rumored to still be carrying on night-time lynchings.

Jenny was becoming more politically aware by 1964. Share-cropping and the land itself had gone steadily downhill since World War II. The family was beginning to move off: Jenny's brothers had joined the Army, two cousins had moved to Chicago, and another had gone to Newark. Black families who left the area first moved to southern cities, then on to border towns like Memphis and Chattanooga, and finally to Detroit, Washington, Chicago, and New York.[2] Letters and occasional visitors from "up North" brought back tales of city life, urban salaries, and welfare benefits.

It was no secret to Jenny's family that this was the big migration of the century. Although Jenny had never had any personal contact with the Student Nonviolent Coordinating Committee (SNCC) or the Congress of Racial Equality (CORE), the political ideas of Martin Luther King's Southern Christian Leadership Conference had reached her through the local Baptist church. It was largely because of her Baptist minister that Jenny and a few of her friends registered and voted for Lyndon Johnson—they had heard of Johnson's poverty program and felt that the government was trying to help them. Jenny, feeling much less politically isolated, help-less, and distrustful, made plans to move North to start a new life. Her cousin in Newark promised Jenny a place to live until she found a job and a place of her own.

By 1968 Jenny's life and ideas had changed considerably. While living with her cousin in a one-room apartment in Newark, she had gotten a job as a maid and married a man who had just returned from Vietnam. His temporary un-employment lapsed into permanent joblessness, and after the first of their children arrived, the periods between welfare checks were filled with tense domestic struggles. After two years of a bitter marriage, Jenny's husband left, and Jenny became inured to regular visits from the social worker, long halls and long lines of government bureaucracy, and her own lies "about no boy friends livin' in."

Political Alienation

Jenny voted for Hubert Humphrey in the 1968 election, but she had little of the conviction or hope of 1964, and she claims she voted partly out of fear that if she didn't the welfare worker might find out and somehow cancel her checks. With the election of Richard Nixon, the death of Martin Luther King, and her own adjustment to the status of being a single parent, Jenny found herself becoming more and more distrustful and worried. There were drugs in the local elementary school, broken glass littering the sidewalk, garbage uncollected in the doorways, and several people had been beaten and robbed coming home from work. Newark no longer seemed a safe, secure, or worthwhile place for her children to live. Yet she had no guarantee of welfare or work anywhere else. Even so, she was thinking about making a long visit "home" to Arkansas, maybe to stay. She felt trapped and looked back with anger at her hopes of 1964, her belief in government, and her faith in Kennedy and Johnson, city life, and welfare benefits. She and many of her friends felt cheated. Had it not been for her regular visits to church, she says she would have found it difficult to find anything to believe in. She certainly didn't vote in 1972 for Nixon or McGovern. There was no point in voting.

Black Alienation

Jenny Jackson represents the most alienated Americans in 1960 and again in 1972. Even though Jenny's situation had changed markedly from her earlier years, and for a time she had found real hope in the promises and programs of sympathetic national leaders during the mid-1960s, the hope had vanished by 1972. Like thousands of other black Americans in similar situations, Jenny's aspirations turned to disillusionment, resentment, and fear. Figure 2-1 shows that in 1960 blacks had been twice as likely as whites to experience all three types of political alienation. During the Kennedy and Johnson

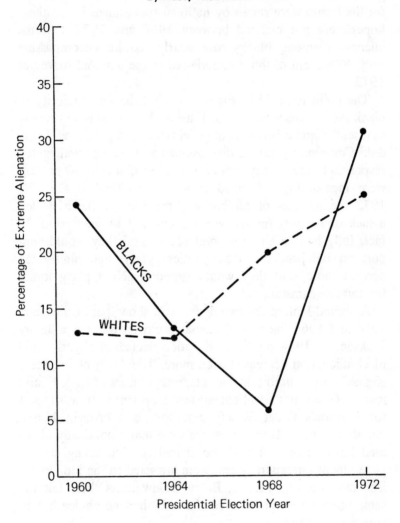

FIGURE 2-1.
Percentage of Extreme Alienation
by Race, 1960-1972

years, this estrangement declined markedly, as expectations for the future were raised by national spokesmen. When these hopes were not realized between 1968 and 1972, extreme alienation among blacks rose nearly sixfold, encompassing fully 30 percent of those interviewed in the national survey of 1972.

The point is made in Figure 2-2 that the vast majority of black Americans were also disillusioned, and many felt nearly as resentful and mistrustful of government and politics as Jenny did.[3] Combining both the disillusioned and extremely alienated responses to the nine questions, it is clear that over 90 percent were measurably estranged from the political system. By 1972 the answers of all but 8 percent of blacks indicated a lack of support for the government and its leadership. In fact, fully half of the alienated blacks said they would support an independent black political party, and almost 25 percent more said they would support such a party under the right circumstances.[4]

A second look at the two figures will show that in the years 1964 and 1968 the typical alienated citizen was not a Jenny Jackson. In 1964 political alienation decreased slightly, and black alienation decreased even more. The death of President Kennedy hit so hard that the integrative forces of tragedy and fear of Goldwater's welfare austerity evidently drew support for Johnson's Great Society ambitions and brought him a landslide victory. However, there were many politically alienated individuals in 1964 who feared the increasing size of government bureaucracy and were attracted to the individualism and outspokenness of Barry Goldwater. Others felt the same uneasiness, yet believed that they had no choice but to vote for Johnson.

Joyce and Ralph White

Joyce and Ralph White typify the politically integrated and optimistic voter of the late-Eisenhower era who became dis-

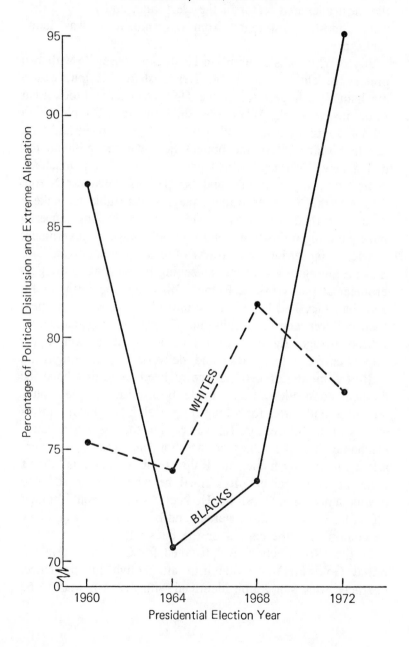

FIGURE 2-2.
Percentage of Political Disillusion and Extreme
Alienation by Race, 1960-1972

enchanted with government by 1964. In 1968 they were in the most alienated sector of the electorate, and in 1972 they were almost as estranged from government as was Jenny Jackson.

Joyce White was a suburban Kentucky housewife with two preteenage children in 1960. Her husband, Ralph, was a mechanic in a large local garage. He loved cars and took great pride in his work. When the children started junior high school, Joyce went to work in the local post office; and with her first year's salary she bought her own second-hand car and a new dryer and helped pay off the washing machine.

In 1960, Joyce, Ralph, and his parents voted for Nixon. This was the last year Ralph's parents were able to make a go of it on their small farm outside of town. Feeling squeezed out by the big farms that could take advantage of government subsidies, by letting large tracts of land go uncultivated, or make a killing in good years by selling huge crops to the government at parity prices, Ralph's folks sold the farm for far less than they had hoped. They moved into town to be near their children and grandchildren. Though nearing mandatory retirement age, Ralph's father took a job at a farm supply depot, carrying feed sacks and delivering farm equipment.

By the middle of 1963, Joyce realized she didn't have the political connections to be made post mistress; she would remain a mail sorter for a long time. Ralph was having problems with his future, too. He was certain that he was a better mechanic than the others at the shop, and many customers asked for him by name, but Ralph realized that this "didn't make an extra nickel." It seemed he would never advance beyond a mechanic's position. He kept wishing to could branch off on his own and start a garage and body shop, but he knew he couldn't get the capital or the backing.

In the 1964 election, Ralph voted for Goldwater. He admired Goldwater's individualism and rough independence, characteristics that Ralph identified with his own wish to be independent. Ralph tried to convince Joyce to vote for Goldwater, but both Joyce and Ralph's parents voted for Johnson. They were worried that Goldwater might cut back social security benefits. Since Ralph's parents were on the verge of retirement, that would mean almost no money coming in for their old age.

Sometime after the election, Joyce began to wonder whether her post office job was worth all the time she was forced to put in there, especially during school holidays. Yet Ralph kept saying that their money just couldn't stretch far enough, even with two salaries. Ralph was particularly annoyed when his father retired in 1965; he could hardly afford to help his parents who were trying to live on a meager social security check. By 1966 Johnson's poverty and welfare programs had become an additional source of irritation. At the post office, Joyce handed out welfare checks and other benefits to "welfare cheaters" and "able bodied men who sit around instead of trying to get work."

Between 1966 and 1968, the Whites' political frustration mounted steadily. Their second son, after working for a year to save money for college expenses, was drafted the summer before he was to enter the state university. Ordinarily they would have been proud that he was serving—the way Ralph and his friends had served in Korea. But with the fighting in Vietnam, a neighbor's son reported missing in action, and the local newspaper printing articles about rich kids escaping the draft and demonstrating in the streets, Joyce and Ralph were left feeling worried, confused, and exasperated. What's more, the government didn't "even seem to be trying to win this war."

At the same time, the garage began to pressure Ralph to work nights and weekends. There was never any mention of overtime rates, and the small raise he got in 1967 "just didn't amount to anything." When the chance came to drive a cross-country truck route, Ralph quit the garage. Truck driving was "just a job." There were many days away from home that

29

Ralph didn't like and there were long hours of boredom on the road, "but at least the pay was good."

Then came the demonstrations and university uprisings of 1968. Ralph was furious:

> Those long-haired creeps are tearing down buildings and beating up cops, while our son's out there maybe gonna get killed any minute so these weirdos can take a bunch of dope and go half crazy. And after our boy worked a year for that . . . I'm tellin' you I just lose all my faith in them colleges. It's the same with the colored. I'm not against colored people, you understand. But here we are working ourselves half to death so's they can lie around drinkin' up our tax dollars.

In the 1968 election, Ralph and his father decided to vote for George Wallace, even though they knew Wallace couldn't win.[5] Joyce didn't vote at all; by now she resented everything connected with the government.

The Whites don't talk much about politics anymore, and they're likely to turn off the TV when almost any politician appears on the screen. "They're all bums!" Ralph claims. Joyce's opinion of government and politicians is even lower—particularly after she was laid off in the latest "reorganization" of the post office.

Ralph and Joyce find they "can't keep up." Ralph is making more money since he's bought his own trucking "rig," but inflation seems to "eat up" any gains he makes. Neither of the Whites voted in the 1972 election. Ralph was on the road, and Joyce "just didn't get to the polls." They both agree that it didn't make any difference anyway.[6]

The Region and Setting of Alienation

In 1960 southerners, such as Jenny Jackson, and border state residents, like the Whites, were twice as likely to give extremely alienated responses as their counterparts in the rest of the country (see Figure 2-3). Many southerners believed that the South had been written off by the presidential candidates that year. (It would be another eight years before Richard Nixon would develop a "southern strategy.")[7] Nixon and Kennedy appeared to be trying to "out liberal" each other with proposals for big government programs and support for racial integration.[8] "Impeach Earl Warren" signs dotted highways in the deep South, and the Ku Klux Klan was experiencing a modest revival in the "piney woods." [9]

In 1964 Goldwater's appeal to the "forgotten Americans" and to southern sentiments is probably reflected in the dramatic decline in southern and border state alienation. Ralph's vote and his father's weren't in the majority in Kentucky, but Goldwater did carry five southern states. Of course, Jenny Jackson and her friends and other black southerners voted overwhelmingly for President Johnson.

Despite Nixon's southern strategy in 1968, southern alienation was dramatically on the rise, presumably stirred up by Governor George Wallace's impassioned appeals against Great Society welfare handouts and by resentment of the northern, big-city, educated style of prevailing political power.[10] Extreme southern alienation rose still further in 1972, but by that time political disenchantment around the country was rising at an even more rapid rate. Jenny, Ralph, and Joyce were typical of alienated voters in their areas, but thousands of others were scattered around the country.

In 1968 intense alienation was on the rise in every residential setting—in the big cities, in suburbia, and in rural America. New inner-city migrants, like Jenny Jackson, and white city dwellers who had not yet fled to the suburbs had become disillusioned with the promises and benefits of big-city life and with the government's inability to deal with the deterioration and dangers there. Homeowners, like Joyce and Ralph, in the adjacent cities and surrounding suburbs had begun to fear the influx of black families from the rural South and

31

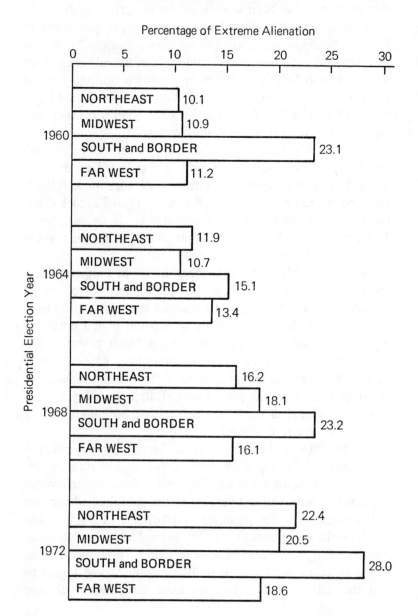

FIGURE 2-3.
Percentage of Extreme Alienation by
Geographic Region, 1960-1972

from the cities' ghettos. The diversity, pace, and troubles of the cities were reaching out into what had once been a placid, all-white preserve. Ralph says he "can't see how anyone would want ignorant coloreds moving in his neighborhood, destroyin' property values, and bringin' all kinds of trouble into the schools."

According to Figure 2-4, urban and suburban alienation climbed rapidly during the late 1960s; rural and small town aversion to national politics was already high, and was climbing still higher. Farmers and other country folks, black and white, who still identified with farming as a way of life, if not as a livelihood, needed no text to know that the nation's vital heart had long since moved to the cities. Politicians had city-slicker styles, and their programs had urban titles. No one seemed to care about country people unless they wanted minimum-wage workers for tough jobs in relocated industries, land for lucrative concessions along the new interstate highways or for lakefront vacation homes, or greater agribusiness profits. Never short on horse sense, rural dwellers weren't likely to miss these trends. Their perception and their anger shows up both in the national statistics and in our interviews.

Ward Beloit

Ward Beloit puts in a tough five- or six-day week "at the mill" in Gary, Indiana. The "mill" is steel, and Ward works on the welding repair crew for twelve plants. For most sedentary Americans, a turn on the swing shift with Ward would be a devastating experience. He's one of the dwindling breed of Americans who thrive on hard physical labor. For relaxation, before and after his shift, on weekends, and during vacations, Ward farms 400 acres of wheat, corn, and soybeans.

Ward has always been a Democrat, and it's his experience that "we seem to have had better times when the Democrats

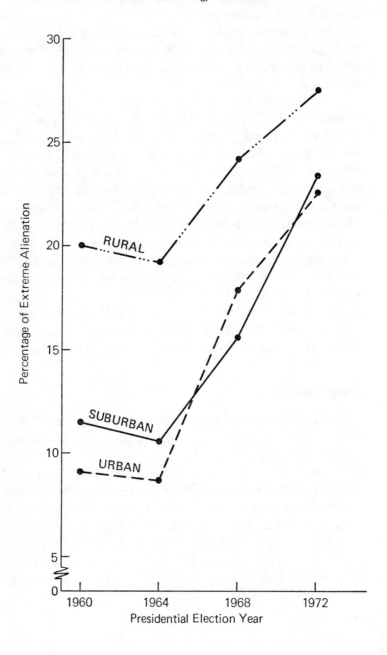

FIGURE 2.4.
Percentage of Extreme Alienation by
Residential Setting, 1960-1972

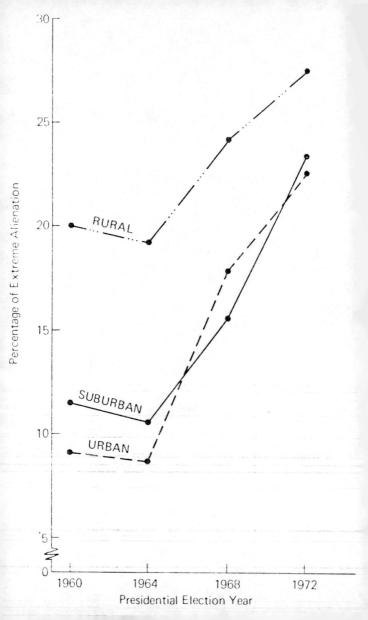

are in office." But Ward's faith in national office holders has been deeply shaken:

They don't really care what I think. It's what they think is best for us that concerns them, and they're always looking out for themselves first. There's a lot of things coming out today that make you think you just can't trust them. Seems like the big businessmen can just walk in and make their price. Politicians just aren't being honest with the public. They seem to be for the minority groups, I mean the big businessmen and the big capital men. They forget the average consumer, the small guy, the men that really make this country work. Shoot, I paid more taxes this year than Nixon has in the last five." *

Ever since he was a kid, Ward wanted to go into farming. His father farmed some, but times were hard then and the family moved around quite a bit—from Gary to Pennsylvania, Ohio, Kentucky, Tennessee, and finally, after Ward's father was killed in a railroad coupling accident in 1946, back to Gary. "My Dad was never really able to find a steady job. He always seemed to think there was something better somewhere else, and I guess most times he was right." Still, it was the farming days that Ward remembers best: "It just seemed like a lot of fun. Even though we did things by hand, it didn't seem as if we had to work as hard as we do now. We went fishing on rainy days, talked with neighbors, and sometimes went to an auction. There was a lot less pressure then. You knew you weren't going to get rich—just like now—but you just didn't worry about it. Now with all the equipment, I think I could use a full-time manager just to keep up with a part-time operation."

Ward was in the service at the time his father was killed, but because it was the postwar army, it was not too difficult to get a hardship discharge. Soon after he was released from

* This comment was made before Congress rendered its decision on President Nixon's delinquent income taxes.

the service, he was able to begin what was only to be one year at the state agricultural school. As far as he was concerned, it was "a total waste of time." He recalls: "Those guys, those teachers up there, didn't even know what a real farm looked like. I guess that's why they were there. Planting alfalfa in between the rows of corn was the big thing they were pushing then. Well, you don't hear much about that these days. It just doesn't work, but they were saying it was the only thing you could do back then." Ward laughingly recalls, "About the only thing I got out of it was meeting my wife there. And I don't know whether it was worth it or not!"

Even with his background and interest, Ward wasn't able to start farming right away—he just "didn't have the capital," and he was married with the first of his children on the way. Ward's wife "wasn't too sure that farm life was for her," so when a good job came up at the mill, he accepted it. Now that Ward has the capital, and his farm operations have already become substantial, he's reluctant to break away from the mill because there's so little time left until retirement. What's more, the risks of farming are normally great, "but those guys in office now sure haven't done much to help the situation any. . . . The thing that disturbs me more than anything in farming," Ward says, "is the shortages and price of fertilizer. The Farm Bureau Federation told us that they were buying fertilizer plants so that the price would come down. Then it was $86 a ton, and just one year later it was $135. Now they don't even know where they're going to start at for the price next season." Ward is just as alarmed at the shortages in equipment: "You just can't get tractors or parts either." In Ward's view, this is all part of the general picture, "and it better change or we'll come to a crashing halt pretty quick. When prices get so high that the little guy can't buy in, then you're gonna see another depression like the 1930s, only worse—unless you figure we can have about 90 percent of the people on welfare."

36

Ward thinks we've simply got to have somebody, probably a Democrat, who can come in and take control of the situation. "I think there has got to be somebody whose character is above question and who can pull it back together, restore our faith. If we could just find a guy like that, then maybe we'd be all right."

Alienation and Occupation

Ward Beloit is one example of the extraordinarily high percentages of industrial workers and farmers who feel thoroughly estranged from their government. More than a third of those who are independent farmers or operatives and workers in American industry and large-scale farms share Ward's distrust for politicians and his increasing feeling of powerlessness to change a national situation he believes to be growing worse. In short, Ward and Ralph White and millions like them are the American workingmen. Robert C. Wood, former under secretary of Housing and Urban Development, describes the workingman as:

> . . . a white and employed male . . . earning between
> $5,000 and $10,000. He works regularly, steadily,
> dependably, wearing a blue collar. Yet the frontiers of
> his career expectations have been fixed since he reached the
> age of thirty-five, when he found that he had too many
> obligations, too much family, and too few skills to match
> opportunities with aspirations.
> This definition of the "working American" involves almost
> 23 million American families.
> The working American lives in the gray area fringes of
> a central city or in a close-in or very far-out cheaper
> suburban subdivision of a large metropolitan area. He is
> likely to own a home and a car, especially as his income
> begins to rise. Of those earning between $6,000 and $7,500,
> 70 per cent own their own homes and 94 per cent drive
> their own cars.

37

94 per cent have no education beyond high school, and 43 per cent have only completed eighth grade.[11]

Peter Schrag terms the workingman " 'the forgotten man,' perhaps the most alienated man in America." [12]

In a similar category, private household workers like Jenny Jackson are also likely to express politically alienated attitudes. As shown in Figure 2-5, 40 percent of the service workers interviewed don't believe in government honesty, the importance of national elections, or their own sense of relevance to the way the government is run. Julio, a lower Broadway short-order cook shook his head when we asked how he voted in 1972: "My vote makes no difference. They're all the same; none of 'em any good." Jim was seventy-one years old last winter, and he's still running the same apartment elevator he helped put into service forty years ago. "It needs replacing," he says, "and I need replacing. But they can't afford it, and I can't afford it." Jim feels much the same as Julio about politicians, "I think they all oughta be kicked out! All they're in there for is the money. But the new ones would probably be just as bad on us or worse." In Springfield, Massachusetts, Shirley, a chambermaid for a large motel says, "No, it doesn't make any difference which party wins; I'll just go on working, same as always."

People like Ward, Ralph, Jenny, Julio, Jim, and Shirley have always been the ones most likely to feel alienated from national politics. This appears to be true not only in America but in other countries as well.[13] They have held jobs that are quite literally at the mercy of wealthy men and of economic forces they could scarcely begin to comprehend. They are even more likely to be alienated now than they were a decade ago. But another and more significant change has taken place among the makeup of the alienated Americans.

Jenny, Joyce, Ralph, and Ward are examples of the most common types of alienation expressed during the 1960s and early 1970s. But with the advent of the Vietnam war, revela-

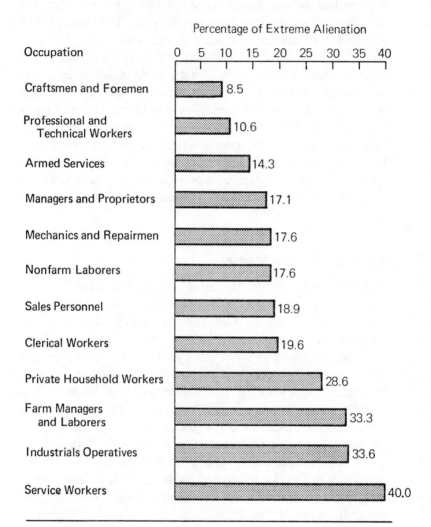

FIGURE 2-5.
Percentage of Extreme Alienation by
Occupational Group, 1972[a]

Percentage of Extreme Alienation

Occupation

| | 0 | 5 | 10 | 15 | 20 | 25 | 30 | 35 | 40 |

Craftsmen and Foremen — 8.5

Professional and
  Technical Workers — 10.6

Armed Services — 14.3

Managers and Proprietors — 17.1

Mechanics and Repairmen — 17.6

Nonfarm Laborers — 17.6

Sales Personnel — 18.9

Clerical Workers — 19.6

Private Household Workers — 28.6

Farm Managers
  and Laborers — 33.3

Industrials Operatives — 33.6

Service Workers — 40.0

[a]Occupational categories are those established by the U.S. Bureau of the Census
and utilized by the ISR questionnaires.

tions of widespread political corruption, and spiraling inflation, disillusionment and despair have spread their roots even into American life situations that can only be described as well adjusted, well heeled, and socially successful. Thus the generally accepted view of political and social alienation in the working class, among those who are most disadvantaged and "oppressed" in modern capitalist societies, must be expanded to include members of the middle class. Throughout our study we found the most vocal expressions of disenchantment and rage voiced by the very people who in years past would have been the government's most ardent defenders: small businessmen, independent entrepreneurs, and professionals who felt they had been betrayed by national policies and political leadership.

Deryl and Sandra Minter

At thirty-one, Deryl Minter is a successful New York attorney in a large corporate firm, with offices near his home in Westchester County as well as in midtown Manhattan. In 1960, during his senior year in high school, Deryl was elated by John Kennedy's election victory. He took it as a sign that the "sluggish, no-nothing" years of the Eisenhower era were over and that a younger, more vigorous, more humane, and socially conscious spirit would reshape politics at home and abroad. He applauded the fledgling Peace Corps and eagerly predicted improved international relations with Asia, Africa, and Latin America and a scaling down of the cold war. In the early 1960s, Deryl participated in the civil rights movement.

In 1974, fourteen years later, Deryl Minter describes the national leadership of both parties as "morally bankrupt." Although he is keenly interested in national and international affairs, he doesn't think it makes "a damn bit of difference" which party wins an election; the *man* makes the difference.

Despite Deryl's legal training, experience, and growing success, he feels that he would be kidding himself to suppose he really knows what's going on in Washington. The government has become so "immense in size and complex in operation" that Deryl feels powerless to influence what he considers to be the "disastrous policies" there.

Deryl cast his first vote in 1964 against Senator Goldwater, whom he saw as the arch opponent of peace and a humane welfare system for the poor and disabled. He didn't see how anyone could "exactly warm up to Johnson," but at the time he viewed the party choice offered him as "crystal clear" and Johnson's programs as "necessary half measures" until something better could be made politically feasible.

Vietnam's political and moral impact hit Deryl with full force. He had married in 1965, and his wife's outspoken anti-war sentiments coincided with his already consuming outrage at America's aerial bombardment of Asia and the massive buildup of U.S. ground forces there. Protest demonstrations in Washington and down New York's Fifth Avenue were eagerly joined by both Minters as a matter of conscience. Shortly after President Nixon's invasion of Cambodia, Deryl and Sandra spent their vacation writing letters urging residents in the hamlet surrounding their vacation resort to protest. But looking back, Deryl regards these moral outbursts, while necessary at the time, as "almost pointless for what they accomplished." They didn't stop the war, and, in the Minter's view, Nixon's "peace with honor" four years later was an "outrageous lie."

In 1968 Deryl had hoped for a Gene McCarthy miracle. After watching that year's Democratic Convention in anger and disgust, he voted for black comedian Dick Gregory. Sandra voted for Humphrey and apologized for it later. Four years later, both Minters voted for George McGovern, without conviction that he could change anything if elected and without a prayer that he could win.

41

Political Alienation

Although Deryl continually criticizes the system in political discussions with friends, he is the first to recognize that he has done quite well within it. Since becoming a partner in the firm last year, his annual income has reached the $30,000 mark. Sandra is doing well, too. After graduation from an excellent college, she worked for a time while Deryl finished law school. Eventually, she went back to school to do graduate work in education. This extra effort has paid off: Sandra has an "exciting" teaching position in a local elementary school and increases the family income by more than $10,000 a year.

In spite of their considerable success, their comfortable suburban home, and their bright prospects for the future, the Minters are among the harshest and most piercing critics of American political life, and they score in the highest percentage of political alienation according to two of the three scales we have used. A glance at Figure 2-6 shows that among those in the upper income bracket, the Minters are not alone in these feelings. Over 14 percent of the $15,000-and-above category are found in the most extremely alienated group in 1972. Among those earning between $6,000 and $15,000, even more were likely to be highly alienated, as many as 20 percent. The fact that there is an increasing degree of political alienation in both high and low income groups is remarkable. These feelings are clearly far more widespread throughout the income range than they were a decade ago. When feelings of both moderate and extreme alienation are combined, as shown in Figure 2-7, the extent of political alienation assumes alarming proportions. The lower income categories approach 90 percent, and even the most comfortable category of income earners exceeds 68 percent in its disillusionment with national politics. This advancing trend of the more affluent and better educated persons in society now begins to challenge the well-documented generalization that those of higher socioeconomic status in society are less likely to developed cynical and distrustful attitudes toward politics.[13]

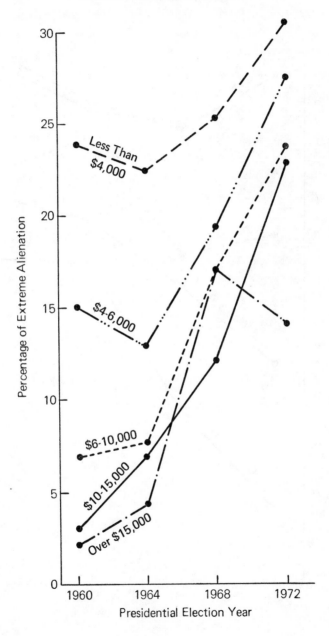

FIGURE 2-6
Percentage of Extreme Alienation by Annual Family
Income (in dollars), 1960-1972

FIGURE 2-7.
Percentage of Political Disillusion and Extreme
Alienation by Annual Family Income, 1960-1972

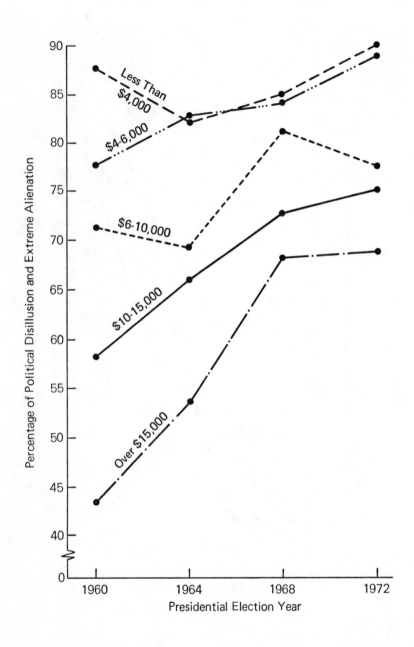

Sherman and Tricia Woods

Sherman Woods is an example of a different group expressing disdain, even contempt, for national politics. Sherman
has another year before he turns thirty. While he is only two
years younger than Deryl, Sherm's view of the future is quite
different. Sherman once hoped for financial success but has
put those thoughts behind him. He spent two years in business school, which for him was pure torture. Then came the
Vietnam war and Sherman was drafted into the Marine Corps
for two years. "No one gets drafted into the Marines," he had
thought. It was tough, but at times Sherman can reminisce
fondly with his Marine buddies over a couple of beers. Sherm's
wife, Tricia, takes another view: "We promised we'd never
forget how awful it was—Paris Island, being separated, never
knowing when you'd be called out, South Carolina—I haven't
forgotten."

Business opportunities weren't good when Sherman was released in 1967, but he had always been handy and construction jobs were available near his home town in Connecticut.
Sanding and sealing floors, that was the ticket: good pay and
none of the tedium of office work. "But $125 a week didn't
go anywhere; all of a week's pay going for rent on a cracker-
box house, more than that for food, car payments, bills, and
nothing left."

In June, as the coming summer began to overheat the old
colonials under restoration and the vapors of floor-sealing
compounds became all but unbearable, the inevitable question was blurted out: "Where is all this getting us?" After a
feverish night packing, Sherman, Tricia, and one-year-old
Abigail "split" for the family place in Maine, where a clear-
ing in the woods, permission to build, and a promise awaited
them.

Pictures in Sherman's album show a log cabin being built
taller at the same time that his hair gradually lengthened and

the stubble on his chin emerged as a full beard by summer's end. Neighbor's remarked on the "hippy types" who were building "up the hill." After a drafty winter in a half-abandoned house and most of another wet summer in a tent, the cabin was ready, the newly established garden showed signs of real production, and a new life was underway.[14]

Sherm figures he's luckier than most. Many of his friends waved goodbye to "straight jobs" at about the same time that he did. But they're still on the move, traveling by thumb, by jammed VW bus, or in whatever way they can manage, criss-crossing the country, Canada, and often Europe in search of a safer haven from society. Others remained at home, staying at dull jobs, switching to other dull jobs, hoping that "some-day" they could get away or somehow get "back" to a more satisfying life somewhere else.[15] Sherman and Tricia's latterday homesteading has by no means solved their continuing money problem. But odd jobs, occasional carpentry, and handicrafts have helped to make a do-it-yourself lifestyle possible.

A few of Sherman's friends were involved in "movement" politics.[16] Don, for example, worked for a while with the Berrigans in the antiwar struggle.[17] Bonnie spent a few months carrying petitions for the Committee to Impeach the President. Sherman hasn't "had time for heavy politics," but like almost all his friends, he thinks that government is dominated by "big capitalists" and moneyed interests who don't care about anyone but themselves. Still, Sherman votes regularly, and, in fact, even ran for a town office one year and made a respectable showing. Tricia serves on the local Democratic Committee. But on the national level, neither thinks that votes or letters to congressmen "really do any good." Some of Sherman's friends say that presidential elections are absurd and a farce. Sherman generally agrees.

Education and Alienation

Sherman and Tricia are among a rising class of Americans who are formally overtrained for what they do. Like the unemployed physicists from Cape Canaveral, Florida, and Houston, Texas, who became auto mechanics and the like, Sherman's business training exceeds his needs as a handyman and some-time metal craftsman. Jobs appropriate to the technical specialties and highly developed skills of such people are either unavailable or uninviting.

Sherm and Tricia have succeeded in a way that differs from Deryl and Sandra Minter. They've learned to simplify and to do without material things that they used to believe were important. Still, their hard cash income is low, bordering on the poverty line, and even though they grow or make a great deal of what they consume, food stamps have saved them from time to time.

Tricia's desire to continue her education and get a college degree in secondary education has also created a strain. Not only is money a problem, but all the country chores must be taken care of before she dashes twenty miles to classes. And now that her degree is in sight, prospects for a "paying job around home" in an "awful teaching market" are not good. The Woodses, then, score high on education, low on income, and high on political alienation of all types.

Although income and education are closely associated in America, Figure 2-8 partially reflects an increasing number of young Americans, like the Woodses, who have been denied the rewards that their educations seemed to promise them or who have rejected the lifestyles that their educational achievement might have obtained for them.

Some of the most important changes in American opinion, then, have been taking place among the best educated and more affluent levels of society, among men and women like Deryl and Sandra Minter. In 1960 political estrangement of managers and professionals was negligible, but in 1972 more than 10 percent of this elite occupational group expressed feelings of extreme alienation. Another 58 percent offered mixed responses of political disillusionment, show-

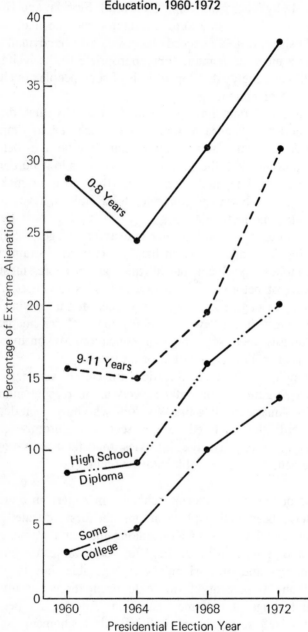

FIGURE 2-8.
Percentage of Extreme Alienation by Years of Formal Education, 1960-1972

0-8 Years

9-11 Years

High School Diploma

Some College

Percentage of Extreme Alienation

Presidential Election Year

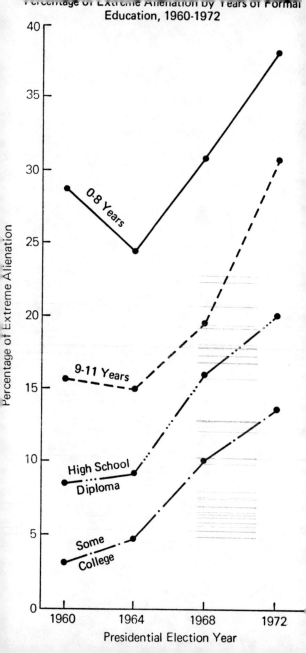

Percentage of Extreme Alienation by Years of Formal Education, 1960-1972

0-8 Years

9-11 Years

High School Diploma

Some College

Percentage of Extreme Alienation

Presidential Election Year

ing at least moderate alienation from a system that had benefited them the most. Others, like Sherman and Tricia, found jobs in the white collar business or professional worlds to be unappealing, personally confining, or unavailable. They've dropped out to an alienated fringe where distrust and contempt for national politics and policy are intense and unrelenting.

chapter 3

More Alienated Americans

Judith Weissman

Three years ago Judith and Howard Weissman moved from the East to a small Oregon town two hours from Portland. Howard was able to find a new teaching job after having "a rough time of it back home; too much of a rat race and not enough money to make a real go of it with the kind of life-style you have back there." The Weissmans' new home is quite modest, and, according to some of the neighbors, the decor is highly individualized, off beat. "But we're out of the suburban thing now," Judith says. The Weissmans' house is set apart from most of the others in town, and there's plenty of open space and room for a large garden in the backyard. In addition to being close to Portland, the Weissmans are near enough for day trips to the Pacific Coast and within easy reach of the mountains as well.

Judith and Howard are in their mid-thirties now, and Howard says that, all things considered, life is treating them "about as well as can be expected." Still, they look back with nostalgia and longing at their pictures of one summer fifteen years ago when Judith was bikini slim and Howie was at his "climbing weight" for taking on the High Sierras. But those

50

days are many pounds and belt sizes away. The Weissmans just aren't as active now either physically or politically. Judith does get out every other week for her "women's group," with its frank talk and fervent plans for opening a new women's medical center. But she says she has always been a bit skeptical of "women's liberation" and to some extent still is. At first the group was welcome relief from the drudgery of household routine. But now that Judith's services as a substitute teacher in the nearby union high school are more and more in demand, even those meetings seem to be an increasing burden. Certainly she doesn't regard them as "real politics."

There was a time in the early 1960s when both of the Weissmans were much more involved in politics. Howard had worked hard as a staff coordinator in the Bronx for the Kennedy campaign. Later he took a position with the New York State Civil Rights Commission. He remembers those times "as if they were yesterday" and "as a time when we really believed we could get things accomplished." But "somehow, after the assassination of JFK, after we got so quickly involved in Vietnam, I just lost my yen to follow through, to go on down to Washington."

Judith remembers being interested in the Kennedy campaign of 1960, but she didn't become actively involved. Kennedy's assassination, though, is still a painful memory, and one that colors her political views today [1]:

I was in Boston, hoping to land a job with a touring theater company. Dancing was my passion then, and it had been since little girl's ballet lessons.

Speak of being lost; I've never felt that way in my life. I took a plane right back to New York to be with Howard. Something like that had never happened in my generation. Nothing, nothing that bad had anything to do with the America I knew anything about. Kennedy was the first president who ever really spoke to me. I really listened to him, and because of him politics began to be meaningful to me. I remember

51

sitting there with Howard just listening to that drum
beat rolling and rolling.

Though they didn't "take part" in the political campaign
of 1964, Judith and Howard both voted for Johnson without
hesitation, knowing that Senator Goldwater was challenging
much of what they and their parents held valuable. After all,
Judith's father had escaped from Poland, almost literally out
of the path of Hitler's invading armies. To them FDR, the
New Deal, and the war against Hitler and the pogroms were
not to be forgotten. Goldwater's "black and white" understanding of the world was "just a bit crazy" and "scary."
Echoes of Lyndon Johnson's thunderous presidential victory
had hardly faded before America seemed to be launching "an
Asian pogrom of its own." During the early troop buildup,
Howard wrote letters of protest to Senators Jacob Javits and
Robert Kennedy. Judith didn't. She felt it was "hopeless to
protest," and subsequent events "proved me right."

In 1968 the Weissmans voted for Senator Eugene Mc-
Carthy in the Democratic primary, even though they didn't
really think he would get the nomination. Howard thought
that the Democratic Convention in Chicago was a "ghastly
business," but he decided to vote for Hubert Humphrey, re-
membering that he "had been one of the strongest liberals
in the Senate." As far as Judith was concerned, "he didn't
deserve anybody's support." Judith says that she "really felt
that Humphrey was a little mass of springs, and if anything
went wrong he'd just go 'twang.' I kept thinking of Humphrey
on the end of a hotline, and it just wasn't right." As for
Nixon, "I couldn't vote for him, of course." Judith stayed
home with the children on election day.

Four years later, Judith was certain that it was impossible
to beat Nixon and "almost as impossible to get any real change
no matter who was President." Nonetheless, she supported
Senator George McGovern in 1972, believing that his "initial
effort was great, even though he didn't hold up."

Judith will probably vote in the next presidential election, though she doesn't expect her vote to make any more difference than it has in the past. As far as she's concerned, she would rather not think about politics: "It's too discouraging." She lumps national politics together with many of the other things she had hoped to leave behind in the city and suburbs: "Keeping up with the Joneses, being coated with all kinds of cars, the money, the materialistic things. At least here I have a choice—trees, birds, and the outdoors."

Alienation and Women

Judith Weissman, like Joyce White and many other women in a variety of situations, became more quickly disenchanted with American politics than did her husband. While Howard still believes that the political system will eventually "pull itself back together," Judith has given up hope and will continue to vote only as a matter of ingrained conscience. Throughout the period of our investigation, women were much more likely to express extreme alienation than were men, nearly twice as likely in the election year 1972, as shown in Figure 3-1. Women have participated less in politics than have men, but women who are interested are far more likely to be estranged from politics as well. This is especially true of women in families earning over $15,000 a year; they were more than twice as likely to feel alienated from politics as were men in similar circumstances.

Many women we interviewed relate their estangement from government to "the position of women in society." This is especially true of those who have been educated beyond high school. Harriet, for example, holds a masters degree in educational psychology but had to disown her advanced standing in order to land a job as a secretary-clerk. She watches helplesly while less-trained men treat her as an office functionary and push by her both in pay and advancement. "This

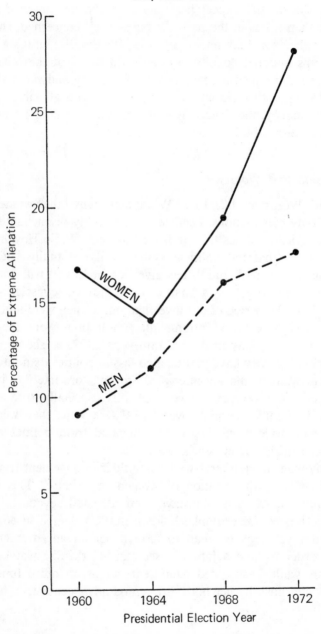

FIGURE 3-1.
Percentage of Extreme Alienation by
Sex, 1960-1972

is all part of the system in this country," she says, "all the way to the very top, with Nixon telling women reporters what to wear at press conferences. How can I respect or believe in a system that treats women like this, like flunkies or slaves?"

Saundra Taylor of suburban Houston is also a college graduate. She did have a promising job before she married, but now she's relegated to "house mistress and babysitter." She'd like to "get a job and do something, be something" besides "just a wife," but her husband doesn't want her to work. Saundra sometimes worries about "feeling the way I do about government, but the whole business is run by men for men. They couldn't possibly know what it's like. I don't know that women would do any better, but I'd sure like to give them a chance to find out."

The inaccessibility of business and professional life for capable, well-trained women has been widely discussed and debated, but the plight of the unskilled and barely educated women—by far the most numerous category—has hardly been explored.[2] The reaction of these women to national politics is striking indeed. Of the women who were unable to complete high school, fully 40 percent expressed feelings of extreme political alienation in 1972. Perhaps this should come as no surprise since society has often discouraged women from continuing their formal education, subtly pointing out that the place for them was in the married household and not so subtly discriminating against them in a host of administrative decisions. Until recently, married or pregnant women were barred from continuing their education in nearly all public schools; counselors encouraged young women to avoid college-oriented courses in favor of secretarial programs; college admissions officers and committees intensified their screening for female applicants. The list of discriminatory practices against women is virtually endless.[3] It may well be that the "undereducated" and often inarticulate women, who are not the Gloria Steinems and Kate Millets of the country, feel an even more justifiable rage about their situations and about the male-dominated national structure that appears to have put them there.[4]

John Shearworth

John Shearworth is the perennial salesman. He's easy to talk to, outgoing, and apparently happy when you first meet him. In truth, John lives a life of not so quiet desperation. He's worked for a number of companies—always as a salesman—selling life insurance, health and accident insurance, encyclopedias, magazine subscriptions, and package tours. All these ventures were entered into with great enthusiasm; none panned out. He traveled from city to city, dragging his family along, but financially he has stood still with little to show for his effort. As John often has told his friends, it was always the guys with the college degrees, the "big money capital," or "the connections" who could get the real chances and the big openings. So for John, life has been a constant promise and a constant disappointment.[5]

John left high school before the end of his junior year, after more than a couple of scrapes with the school administrators and a brush with the juvenile authorities. School was a bore and was too confining, and frequent family moves from one midwestern or southern city to another hadn't seemed to help either his interest or his grades. It was 1951 when John quit school, and he knew that he would soon be drafted to fight in the Korean War. But John was anxious to go. He and two buddies signed up for a three-year hitch in the Air Force.

For John, "Korea" mean Japan, where he remained in the headquarters batallion for most of his hitch. He saw no military action, but there was plenty of activity. John still speaks enthusiastically about his life there and of the Japanese girl who lived with him: she "knew how to treat a man," better than any woman he has known here in the States, including his now estranged wife. All went well until John became implicated in a black market operation involving stolen government property. No formal charges were filed, but John was summarily given a "gray" discharge, not dishonorable but not honorable either.

Home from the service, John dated and finally married his high school sweetheart, and they had two children in rapid succession. John had managed to get his high school equivalency diploma while he was overseas, and for a while he hoped that he might get into college on the G.I. Bill. Yet there never seemed to be enough money to think seriously about it. He did start two correspondence courses, but they never led anywhere. In a short time, his life seemed to drift into sales and his thoughts to more successful pitches and untried deals.

John hadn't much interest in politics until Barry Goldwater appeared and seemed to say just what he had been thinking —that able-bodied men were living off welfare, that more and more useless government bureaucrats and college professors, who really didn't know anything, were running the country. High taxes infuriated John, who kept asking, "After all, what did government ever do for me, personally?" He joined the Citizens for Goldwater Committee early in the campaign, and he was active in canvassing until election day. John's selling ability was so good that he was able to convince most of his friends to participate in Goldwater's campaign. John is still disappointed that Goldwater lost, and he's sure that "the liberal press and the Eastern Establishment smeared him so bad that he couldn't possibly win."

John strongly supported George Wallace in 1968.[6] He saw in Wallace a fighter for the forgotten individual against the whole government machinery. He didn't really think Wallace had a chance, but he gave money and talked to his friends about the need for "law and order" that Wallace could reestablish. Each time Wallace made his hard-hitting speeches on television, John shouted encouragement. "George really

57

put it on the line about those 'pointy-headed intellectuals' and the 'bearded, beatnik bureaucrats!' " In 1972, with Wallace shot and McGovern running against Nixon, John decided to write in for Wallace anyway, to vote his conscience, to foul up the "liberal press," and to make them see that there were "others out here who don't like the choices they're giving us." But when election day came, he decided that it wouldn't make any difference. He didn't bother to go to the polls.

Alienation and Marital Status

John's increasing bitterness about government and law and order seems to stem not only from his being a Horatio Alger who didn't happen. He's been certain all along that if he had the credentials, capital, or contacts things would have worked *for* him instead of against him. Now his anger and cynicism are doubly aroused by his involvement with the legal system in a hotly contested and seemingly endless divorce proceeding. John feels that the laws on separation and divorce are unfair. He feels trapped in his latest job in a city he doesn't like, simply to keep paying his wife what he feels the law unfairly forces him to pay:

> Like in everything else, in this divorce game I'm playing by
> someone else's rules, meeting their requirements, giving
> up everything so that I'm living here in one room like a
> bum after working my whole life. I mean, there's gotta be
> something wrong with a government that has so many
> shyster crooks top to bottom and yet where you spend half
> your life working just to keep your head above water and
> stay within the little yellow line of legality that the cops
> and judges and the politicians are stepping over all the time
> like you see in the paper.

Curiously, John's wife, Janet, feels much the same way and is almost as bitter about her situation and the government as is John.[7]

58

Not all people in limbo before divorce or reunion feel politically alienated like John, who had been chronically out of sorts with national government for years. But for many, the beginning of a divorce proceeding and the period of separation is the first experience with the ways and delays of judicial bureaucracy. Janet, for example, "had never really thought much about politics, despite all that John used to say," but now she's "had time to think about all this, not just Watergate and all, but the whole way it's done." Janet doesn't like what she finds, and neither do many others in her maritally and governmentally estranged position.

In 1972 nearly half the national sample of separated marital partners were extremely alienated politically. The maritally separated were consistently as much or more than twice as likely to express intense political alienation than those who are single, married, or finally divorced. Also, as shown in Figure 3-2, widows and widowers score somewhat higher on the alienation scale, but generally not quite as high as those whose marriages have been broken but not legally severed.[8]

The rapid spread of political alienation is by no means restricted to those who are separated or widowed, rising corporate professionals, long-haired dropouts, feminists, or ne'er-do-wells. In fact, the most typically alienated age group during the past dozen years has been those sixty-five-years and older. One can hardly wonder at this or blame our senior citizens for their disenchantment; they have watched their cherished ideals and accustomed modes of life pummeled by change in a kind of "future shock" of the present.

Alan Arthur

Alan Arthur is sixty-seven this year, and, although he is nearing retirement, he's the one who will set the date and the terms. Al has had a checkered career, scoring successes, then weathering setbacks in a number of false starts. But he "found

59

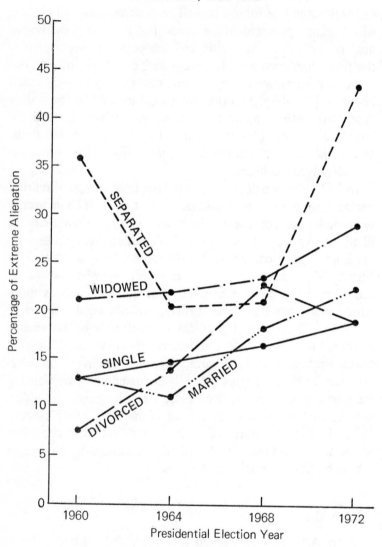

FIGURE 3-2.
Percentage of Extreme Alienation by
Marital Status, 1960-1972

a niche," his way to "beat the game," when he set up his own accounting service nearly twenty years ago. Al and his wife, Jean, have achieved a comfortable standard of living by anyone's reckoning. Yet Al in his attractively decorated California home, no less than Sherman in his rustic north woods cabin, is thoroughly put off by American politics.

It wasn't always this way. At the Depression's nadir, Al cast his first vote for Franklin D. Roosevelt, and he still remembers that "golden voice" on the radio saying, "The only thing we have to fear is fear itself." Al thought of himself as "lucky" during the Depression; he "even got a raise" at the large insurance company where he worked. At the same time, he was able to get a college degree by going to school at night and during the summers. Al voted for Roosevelt again in 1936, but that was to be his last vote for FDR.

By 1939 Al and his new wife saw that America couldn't escape the European conflict. Because of his education and business experience, he was able to enlist as an Army lieutenant. In many ways, wartime was the very height of Al's life: "the world's greatest, brightest young guys working for me," extensive travel, rapid advancement, and immense responsibility for the organization of massive depots around the country to supply both theaters of war. Victory in Europe and Asia was a letdown as the postwar army drifted into its doldrums. "The best men were eager to get out," and Al couldn't wait to get on to other things.

During the late 1940s and early 1950s, Al and Jean watched their carefully hoarded wartime savings be eaten away by inflation and by Al's starting and abandoning several careers: an unpalatable stint with civil service, abortive efforts at sales, and comptrollerships in several small companies. Financial success was elusive.

Al had declined to vote during the war years. He simply regarded Roosevelt as "the commander in chief" and himself as the "subordinate." He meant to vote in 1948, but he was

61

"so sure" that Tom Dewey was a shoo-in over Harry Truman that he didn't bother. As the years passed, both he and Jean maintained an active interest in national affairs. In 1952 he followed the presidential campaign much more closely, and on the urging of friends and family cast a vote for Eisenhower. Al remembers thinking throughout the Eisenhower years that Richard Nixon was a "lightweight" and "a sneak." In 1960 he voted for Kennedy, although he was never very comfortable about Kennedy's untested youth or his "Harvard squad" in the White House.

Al and many of his friends felt reassured by the succession of Lyndon Johnson to the presidency in 1963; he had a good government background and their generation's experience. They felt that Johnson wouldn't "go too fast" on civil rights and that he would be "good for business." This was important both to Al's small business clients and for his own slowly accumulating investments.

Al's one-man accountancy business was doing well by the mid-1960s. Though he was never one to charge what the traffic would bear or aggressively attempt to enlarge his firm with a partner or full-time employees, his gross earnings were nearing $15,000 a year. Jean, though "hopelessly underpaid" as a bank clerk, made a substantial contribution to an increasingly comfortable middle-class lifestyle, one that could boast of more than an occasional Wednesday afternoon spent golfing and two children successfully launched in college.

Al's satisfaction with the Johnson administration and his grudging tolerance of bigger government in general were swept away by the Vietnam war. Outrage is too mild a term for his state of mind in 1967 and 1968: "the insanity of those liars, butchering a helpless people," the "cowardice of American air attacks on villages and hospitals," the "absurdity of believing you could have 'Great Society' programs and a major war without wrecking the economy with inflation!" After Al's post-World War II experience, he had never held career bureaucrats in high esteem. "Anyone who was worth a damn wanted out as much as I did after the war." Now he was beside himself: "Those lardass numbskulls wallowing in the public trough!"

Al has always regarded wealth as critically important, the "way we keep score in this country." On that level, Al and Jean have done better each year, yet they are vaguely dissatisfied. Al speaks wistfully of retirement to an island somewhere, maybe New Zealand, someplace where genuine independence is possible, away from both the demands and benefits of government. He views American politicians as wholly corrupt and venal.

Alienation and Age

The focus of television and the press on youthful discontent during the past decade may make the extreme alienation of Alan and those of his age group seem unlikely. Senior citizens occasionally protest static social security benefits, but their meager outcries have been constantly upstaged by the dramatic indignation of youth. Nonetheless, as Figure 3-3 shows, Americans over sixty-five have consistently been the most alienated citizens.[9] In contrast, those in the most youthful group, ages eighteen to thirty-four, were typically much less estranged from politics than were their seniors. In fact, the youthful group was found to be the least alienated in 1968, the year of intense Vietnam discontent, the student outburst at Columbia University, and the tumultuous Democratic Convention in Chicago, where hundreds of demonstrators were either arrested, beaten, or both. But an increase in youthful alienation is found between 1968 and 1972, as the waves of student and antiwar demonstrators ran their course and the Nixon administration launched its first term.

The youthful dissent and alienation probed in depth by Kenneth Kenniston and Paul Goodman, among others, were

63

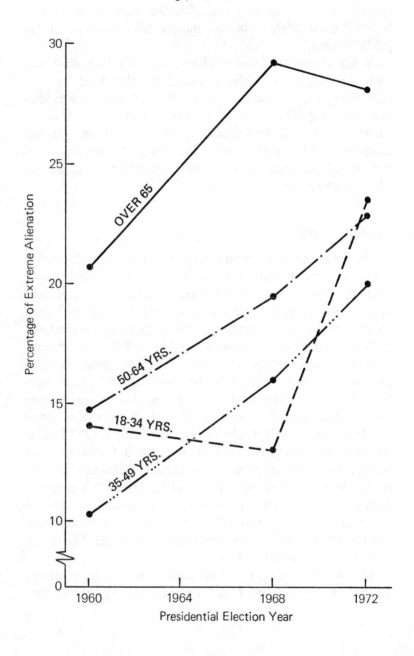

FIGURE 3-3.
Percentage of Extreme Alienation by
Age, 1960-1972

Percentage of Extreme Alienation

30

OVER 65

25

50-64 YRS.

20

18-34 YRS.

15

35-49 YRS.

10

0

1960   1964   1968   1972

Presidential Election Year

genuine in the 1960s and early 1970s and deserved the serious discussion received.[10] What's more, the university uprisings and mass demonstrations in Washington and Chicago could hardly be ignored by contemporary commentators.[11]

In sheer numbers, however, the quiet alienation of the aged is a more impressive story. In 1968 and again in 1972, extreme alienation was the response of nearly 30 percent of Americans over age sixty-five. Some were like Alan and Jean Arthur in the rising group of well-educated and comfortably situated professionals or managers entering retirement. But many more were not so affluent; they were already caught in the squeeze between stagnant social security benefits and double-digit inflation.

Jack Budeau

Jack Budeau is one of those caught in the squeeze. After a lifetime of hard work, farming as a young man, then logging for years in the northern Vermont and Canadian woods, and finally "workin' fer the government in the armory durin' the War an' afterwards," Jack retired thirteen years ago. Actually, Jack never fully retired, and he probably never will. He's constantly at work helping out his rural New England neighbors, mowing their lawns, hauling things that need hauling, or "tinkering up" broken things. Sometimes there's a little pay for his troubles, but other times the work is done simply because "I've got lots of time." For the most part, Jack depends upon his monthly $176 from the Social Security Administration to make ends meet. But there's "one thing," Jack says, "that helped me out in a lot of ways—I'm friendly with just about everybody." Even so, social security and the few extra dollars he earns are stretched thin:

> You've gotta have some savin's; ya gotta pick up every odd
> job ya can, an' watch every penny. I've always burnt more or
> less wood here. I've got a big chunk stove down cellar. But

65

you take, I've gotta pay my taxes; I've gotta pay my lights;
I've gotta pay my fuel for what gas I burn.

This inflation's raisin' hell with me. I can't afford to pay
no $1.75 to $1.95 a pound for meat. Now that propane
gas is up every other month. That fuel business . . . [shakes
his head] and now, what, they gonna jump our electricity
22 to 23 percent.

When my wife was alive, why I'd get her everything she
wanted that I could afford. She used to watch those TV
games in there, an' she had two electric lights goin', then
she had the electric fry pan, an' the toaster. The electric used
to cost about $11 a month. Now I'm alone, an' I don't use
no toaster; the TV's unplugged; I don't use no fry pan.
I use one bulb at a time, an' I gotta pay $15 to $16 a month.

Asked what's causing all this, Jack snaps, "Politics for one
thing!" In Jack's view, "The poor man's just gotta have more
to live on." But as he sees it, "Those big outfits, those big corporations, they figure they've gotta have more profits, so's they
can pay more dividends to their stockholders. And the *poor*
devils, they can't afford to have no stock in anythin' but the
cemetery." As far as Jack is concerned, the politicians aren't
helping the situation a bit: "Are you donatin' for any of them
bastards runnin' for office? I guess you're not! Why, who picks
those politicians; we don't. We just choose one of the ones
they pick. I don't see no difference between 'em. Half of 'em's
crooked, an' the other half oughta be in jail."

Like many senior citizens, Jack looks back with nostalgia
on "better times":

People were happier years ago. These little barns you see
around here—most of 'em had a heifer and a cow. Most of us
had a horse. Roy had one, and I always had one, and we useta
get together to draw wood—one load for one and another
load for the other. Everybody 'round here did that. You wouldn't
remember any of this, but you ever heard of a gramophone?
Well, Parkinses down to the village usta have one, an' on a
Saturday night, we'd all go down ta listen, a whole bunch of us,

just ta listen when they got a new cylinder. The girls even useta
get dressed up, an' we'd have popcorn, maybe some cider. It
weren't anything like your fancy entertainments today, but I
swear we were more contented then.

Jack's bitterness about present conditions is intensified by
his recollections of the way things used to be, especially where
the elderly are concerned:

You take the old days, the children took care of their old
folks. Some maybe didn't fare so well, but they was took care
of. Well, today I never see my children. An' whenever I
do see 'em, they're always acting as if I'm gonna ask 'em for
somethin'. Well, I don't want nothin' from 'em. An'
that son of mine's s'posed to be a big shot. The way it is
now, the government's givin' us a handout half good
enough ta keep goin'. I hope it ain't too far to my station,
til I can get off.

The Graying of America

The coloring of the American future may not be the "greening" or "blueing" that some professors have suggested [12] but
rather a "graying." The average lifespan of Americans may
not be increasing any longer, but the ranks of the pensioners
and social security dependents are growing larger every year.
Americans sixty-five years and over now make up more than
10 percent of the population, and their numbers, both absolutely and relatively, are rapidly increasing. The elderly have
been inescapably buffeted by long lifetimes of unprecedented
change and seasoned in both the prospect and the disappointment of American life. Then, for the most part, they have
been cast aside by family and friends to the isolation of institutional "homes" and retirement communities. The extended
family of yesteryear has become virtually extinct. Jack has
been fortunate to retain his health and vigor long after many
of his friends have lost both and their independence as well.

67

"I ain't got much," Jack says, "but what I got is paid for."

The postwar "baby boom," with its recently bloated statistics of incoming college students and burgeoning work force figures, is now over. The "youth cult" that was so visible in the 1960s is entering middle age; school enrollments are declining; and colleges are entering an era of fierce competition for student enrollments. Many demographers confidently predict a continuing decline in the national birth rate, reaching zero population growth by the end of the century. The evident effect of these trends is that a diminishing working population will have to bear the increasing burden of welfare payments for larger and larger numbers of their retired elders. If, as many suggest, social security benefits become tied to the cost of living index, monthly or weekly pay check deductions are likely to become far more burdensome than they are today.[13]

Neither the direction of these shifts in the population characteristics nor their implications for public policy appear likely to be headed for reversal in the near future. More mature and elderly Americans have traditionally been more likely to vote and otherwise take part in American politics than their juniors. Nonetheless, the elderly have consistently been more politically disillusioned and alienated. As the mode of the population becomes older, then, the politically significant "cult" of the future may well be the cult of the aged and politically estranged. There is no reason to assume that the senior citizens groups of tomorrow will be the frail and timorous ones of the past.

chapter 4
The Decline of Allegiance

THE SHARP RISE in the numbers of extremely alienated Americans is nearly a mirror image of the declining allegiance to American politics. Even so, many people still supported the government and national leaders during the Watergate disclosures of 1973 and 1974. In the midst of the House impeachment proceedings against President Nixon in 1974, as much as 20 percent of the citizenry expressed support for Nixon at the same time that his strongest bulwarks collapsed and the legions of his influential and even his conservative-minded accusers multiplied. Others dropped their support of the Nixon regime but maintained their allegiance to the American political system. Indeed, some saw Watergate as a convincing demonstration of the system's strength and self-purification. In 1972, according to our combined scales, before Watergate had begun to make its heaviest impacts, nearly 21 percent of the national sample held a strongly positive view of the system.

In broad strokes we could sketch the system's faithful, the politically "well integrated" and allegiant, as the other side of the coin from the estranged Jennys, Joyces, Ralphs, and Jacks. Those most likely to believe in government responsiveness, honesty, and representativeness are the ones who have consistently been its prime beneficiaries. An increasing number of successful professionals, like Deryl Minter and Alan Arthur, have lost faith and defected, but many, if not most, of these educated and prosperous men and women have retained their belief and their hope, as one small town banker put it, that "everything will straighten out again soon."

While the stalwart supporters of the national political system have been likely to succeed financially and organizationally, they are no longer as likely to be the traditional pillars of society in their communities. They simply haven't the time to be—they are not in any one place long enough. Over the back fence, an IBM electronics engineer in Boca Raton, Florida, makes the point quite plainly: "It's a beautiful town, I love my home here, and I'd really like to be active in things. I felt the same way while we were in White Plains. But I know I'll have to move in two or three years, and there's nothing I can do about it." America's elites are increasingly transients, strangers, or "short-timers" in their erstwhile "hometowns" and are hard pressed to tell you where they're really "from." [1]

Vance Packard observes that "personal isolation is becoming a major social fact of our time. A great many people are disturbed by the feeling that they are rootless or increasingly anonymous, that they are living in a continually changing environment where there is little sense of community." [2] The sheer amount of residential movement would appear to make such conclusions inevitable:

> About 40 million Americans change their home addresses
> at least once *each year*. And more than a third of these
> people move across the county or state line. In this twen-
> tieth century there has been a 25 percent increase in
> people living in a state other than the one in which they were
> born. That is only mildly suggestive of the amount of
> total movement that has actually been occurring. . . .
> During the twenty-year period from the 1940 Census to the
> 1960 Census there was a leap of 50 percent in such
> internal migration.[3]

70

This continual motion may well result in "a nation of strangers," isolated and *socially alienated*. But these same people often do not feel political powerlessness, meaninglessness, and distrust of national government. The passage of these affluent pilgrims is tied directly to the national system of economic affairs and national corporation policies.[4]

Of course, not all of those who still have a strong belief in American government are itinerant organization men who have little opportunity or energy left over for community affairs. Almost every community still has its established professionals and home-grown entrepreneurs with a yen for local politics and affairs. Despite the tremendous number of corporate mergers and takeovers, and the seemingly unending trend toward thoroughgoing governmental control of business operations, nearly 15 million private businesses remain in America. The men who create and operate these enterprises have declined in numbers and importance, but they are still widely regarded as appropriate models for American identity and success.[5]

Byron Vining

Byron Vining calls himself a "conservative," and he believes the country has always been basically conservative. "That's what made the American Revolution different from revolutions in all those other places; it's what made this country great. It wasn't done by a bunch of radicals with foreign ideologies. It was done by conservative men who had a lot of common sense."

Byron now heads the insurance and investment realty company his father founded and ran until his health began to fail some ten years ago. Initially, the firm only handled insurance, but early on Byron recognized the emerging boom in second-home and vacation property, and he moved aggressively to meet the growing demand. From offices in Savannah, Georgia,

71

he now controls real estate development operations spanning the Southeast, from the North Carolina mountains to the Florida Keys. Byron is especially proud that he had the right idea and acted on it, "without a lot of dallying around. . . . buying up those worn out hill farms, bringing in the surveyors, and creating whole new communities up there in the mountains. Now we've got what we call 'lookin' out lots' of about a quarter acre, 'dreamin' lots' of maybe half an acre, and real substantial building lots of one or two acres. We've got a lot of houses going in on our North Carolina property and a good number of them already completed. There's wonderful people livin' up there now."

These activities have brought Byron and his firm under increasing pressure from local environmental groups and governments, but he feels prepared for them. "I'm a conservationist myself," he claims.

It's just these wild-eyed liberals who keep pushing everything too far. Take this Alaska pipeline thing, for example. It's really a question of, do you want to protect a bunch of bugs and snakes up there in places nobody has ever seen, or do you want some oil to run your cars and keep the country going? I think we've got enough bugs and snakes already.

Why, I was a conservationist before any of these fellas ever heard the word. Just let me give you an idea. Over five years ago, I put in an exclusive development down on the Bay. We had barely gotten these fine homes completed when we found soot ash coming down all over everything from the power plant down there. Every morning the roofs and patios were black from that stuff. Well, I got together with John Anders and a couple of other fellas doing business down that way; we got the facts and just laid it on the line up in Washington. You'd better believe they listened. Why, they were planning to enlarge that plant, and before we got done, we forced them to move the whole thing further down the coast. You know a plant like that doesn't have any business being there in a fine neighborhood like ours.

Let me give you another example. We had an important waterfront development going on down in the Keys. The canals were dug, and the foundations were being poured. Then the state commission of something or other of the environment came around to enforce regulations they had just finished making—so new the ink wasn't hardly dry. Well, you know, they made us wait four months—holding up everything, losing thousands of dollars every day—while they carried on their "studies." Then they held a public hearing at the Capitol, and I'll be damned if they hadn't gotten it all completely screwed up, forgot to do half of what they were supposed to do. They were the biggest fools I've ever seen. They hadn't done a thing on the sewerage study they were supposed to complete: standing up there asking each other who was in charge of it. They didn't even know they hadn't done anything until we raised the question. We went ahead with construction the next week. We knew it was a good project, and there wasn't a damn thing they could do about it.

Byron is quite pleased about the fact that, although he decided to leave college during his sophomore year, he is now on the board of trustees of the small denominational school he briefly attended. He wields considerable influence, not only in their fund-raising drives for capital plant expansion but also in the improvement of their library, faculty, and scientific facilities. He is also an active member and past president of one of the local business clubs. What's more, he's a strong family man and insists "that's the most important thing in my life after business." He "suffered an awful lot" during the breakup of his first marriage, "but now that's all over"; he has the children and a new wife.[6] He enjoys taking his family out in bracing weather, sailing along the coast in his forty-two-foot yawl. Although they sometimes protest that it's too rough, he's pleased at the end of the day when they're tired but glad they went. "I take *all* my responsibilities seriously, just the way I take my responsibility to government seriously, *when* I think it's doing the right thing at the right time and in the right way."

Besides using the more direct forms of influence, Byron is a conscientious voter. He was an enthusiastic and generous supporter of Richard Nixon, whom he regarded as "sound" and "somewhat like me, on the conservative side." This support lasted only until Byron realized that Nixon just couldn't get the job done anymore. He felt that Nixon should have resigned as soon as he couldn't run things. "That's the way it would be in business."

If there is anything really wrong with government generally, Byron says it is laziness and inefficiency. He thinks it is the same in business, but not half as bad. And at least he can deal with that: "It's very important for me to get my men in at least once a week for briefings from the top. They've got to get it straight that we've got to hussle, and we can't afford to slack off or make stupid mistakes. I really prepare for those talks because I know that $10,000 or $15,000 rides on every one of them. Well, that's the way we ought to have it in government, and there's no reason we couldn't."

Byron is outspoken in his opinions on his country: "It's a great country, and most of our problems have been blown up all out of proportion by the northern press." From his point of view, "These snivelling liberals ought to be damn glad they live here instead of some of the God-forsaken places I've seen. This is the greatest country on earth, and we ought to be damn proud of it!"

Affluence, Age, and Allegiance

Byron is a good example of the many men who have succeeded in the American system and who extend their robust support in return. Like Byron, some of those who have done exceptionally well had a good start—a place in the family business or strong family backing for ventures of their own. Others began careers at auspicious locations in the public or private bureaucracies destined for rapid growth, such as the military or large-scale private business. Many others, of course, view a man like Byron as the epitome of the entrepreneurial success they hope to attain but probably never will.

For the most part, financially successful people are more likely to trust national political leaders and to feel that there is genuine significance in the choices offered them by the political party system. Though they normally wouldn't have accumulated as much money as Byron, and on the average probably couldn't exert nearly as much political influence as he does, they tend to feel that their voices matter politically and that the government is responsive to their needs.[7]

Figure 4-1 clearly shows this general sentiment, especially among those who earn over $15,000 a year. In 1960, half the people in this highest income bracket expressed strong support for the political system; only about 2 percent felt politically alienated. But this situation has obviously changed dramatically over the past decade and a half. As extreme alienation has increased by multiples of five to seven among the most affluent groups, allegiance to the system in the same categories has fallen precipitously.

A look at the various age groups of Americans in terms of strong belief in the system is also revealing. Like Byron, those at the age of generally greatest material success and productivity (thirty-five to fifty) are most inclined to be strong believers in the performance of American politics. Figure 4-2 displays this peak in system support among the middle-aged group in 1972 and also the marked decline in citizen faith in the system's performance as age increases.[8] In 1972 less than 15 percent of men and women over age sixty-five maintained a strong belief in the system. A closer look at Figure 4-2 shows that most Americans do not hold extreme beliefs in the system nor are estranged from it. In fact, the percentage of

FIGURE 4-1.
Percentage of Strong Political Allegiance and Extreme
Political Alienation by Annual Family Income, 1960-1972

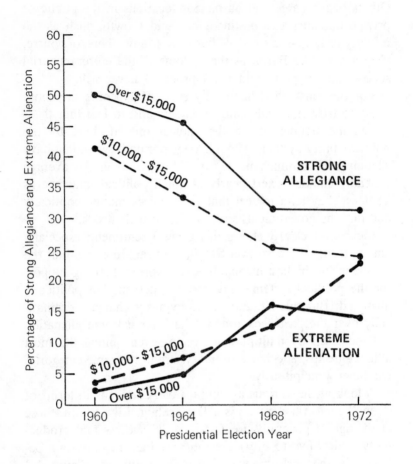

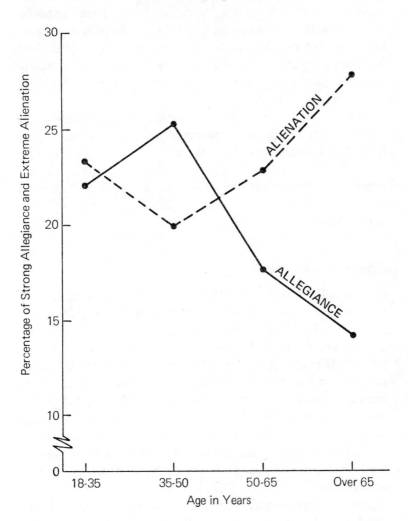

FIGURE 4-2.
Percentage of Strong Political Allegiance and Extreme Political
Alienation by Age, 1972

people at all age levels who express mixed or disillusioned reactions to national politics, partially alienated and partially still accepting and believing, has been a relatively consistent majority. But it is curious to observe that the rate of decline in strong allegiance to the American political process is nearly the same as the rate of increase in extreme alienation as age advances beyond fifty.

Those with American-style success stories, responding at an age when careers promise maximum achievement and meaning, are still much more likely to support the political system than those who never tasted the comfort of higher income brackets and whose careers are on the wane or over. Yet, even among the affluent and productive, there have obviously been many defectors.

Arnold Dryden

Arnold Dryden is not a defector, and he probably never will be unless the system abandons him in some economically dramatic way. By his own description, Arnold says, "I guess I'm a real company man." He's been with General Foods Corporation nearly twenty years, having joined the company right after college. Arnold went directly into junior management training, worked his way up in the division handling the company's dog food, and finally "switched over to cereals." He's still proud of the record his division made while he was there: he capitalized on the widely advertised need for "real meat" in the dog food products by making the project economical in production. He feels he had a big hand in that success.

Since college, Arnold and his wife Emily have moved four times with the company—to California, New Jersey, Illinois, and then to Michigan, his "home state." Despite these moves, the Dryden's "always seem to fit right in with the new set of people" wherever they are. Emily invariably finds a ready welcome with the local bridge club, the garden group, and the school PTA. "There always seem to be people like us, and it just doesn't seem to be any problem at all," Emily says. At each stop the Dryden's have had a new or nearly new suburban home that they found with help from the company or with the assistance of professionals. "Every neighborhood has been just about right for us," Arnold recalls, "with many of our neighbors also with the company or with other substantial firms in the area. Oh, that one town in Jersey was a can of worms—with the Mafia running it and all—but even there our own neighborhood was pretty good. And here in Grand Rapids, you just can't beat it for clean living."

Now that Arnold is "in cereals," he's definitely on his way up in middle management. He's gotten "really involved in the business" and is constantly on the look out for "new ways to improve production and distribution systems." Arnold has only recently gotten in on the sales end of the business and feels he's "finally getting the big picture." [9]

Arnold hasn't "spent that much time worrying about Watergate," but he does remember being "really upset" about the congressional investigation of breakfast cereal nutrition: "It was completely unfair!" He feels somewhat vindicated that, after months of investigation, the whole case was allowed to drift into oblivion. Still, he says, "They should have admitted they were wrong and made that clear." Since he's always thought of himself as a Republican, it bothered him a good deal at first that such an "irresponsible" inquiry would have been begun under a Republican administration. At length, he concluded it was the Democratic Congress that did the actual investigation, just to stir up trouble.

Arnold rarely attends political meetings except when they are directly connected to his work.[10] Yet he did attend a Nixon rally in Illinois along with several other young executives. He also made a modest pledge to the 1972 Nixon campaign fund, just as he had done in 1968. Emily says she never does "anything more political than go to the PTA," yet she and her husband always vote, and they are avid Republicans.[11] Their parents were also Republicans, and they followed suit, as Arnold tells it, "because the Republicans are good for business and the country, and the Democrats aren't." Just as the presidential impeachment proceedings began in the early summer of 1974, Arnold resolutely stuck a "Get Off His Back!" sticker beside the "Nixon Now" sticker still attached to his Oldsmobile bumper.[12]

Generally, Arnold believes "there's too much government interference with private business, but all in all, government probably does a pretty fair job."[13] As far as he's concerned, "Nixon was unfairly attacked by minority groups, and especially by labor unions and George Meany, because they were out to get him. . . . Nixon's record still looks darned good compared to those labor bosses who just drive up the cost of wages and create inflation." Arnold says he can "half believe" that the whole Watergate affair was a plot by "the press and Democratic minority groups" to "ruin Nixon and kick all the other decent Republicans out of office and gain control of the government." But Arnold hopes, "for the sake of the country," that "they won't get away with it." *

Political Allegiance and Participation

Men like Byron and Arnold, who are successful and feel most in tune with national decision makers, are quite likely to hold positive views about the representative strength of national political institutions and the capacity of government to achieve national goals. This comes as no great surprise, but the magnitude of difference between the opinions of these people and those who are most alienated from American politics is remarkable.

When asked "how helpful" the government is in dealing

* Arnold's comments were made before the final disclosures of the Watergate tapes and President Nixon's resignation.

with the most important national problems, the politically supportive respondents, shown in Figure 4-3, were more than three times as likely to reply, "Very helpful," than those who were most alienated. Thinking back to 1972, Arnold says that he had thought the Vietnam war was then "the most important problem." And he believes that "President Nixon did a darned good job in getting us out of there." Others who support the government view the Vietnam situation in the same way as a now retired Coast Guard chief in Miami: "Under the circumstances, we did an excellent job there." In direct contrast are the assessments of most alienated respondents. For Deryl Minter and Alan Arthur the Vietnam war and "peace with honor" were "insane butchery" and an "outrageous lie." John Shearworth thinks "the whole thing was a farce. We should have bombed them off the face of the earth." Either way, there is little support among the most alienated for the government's middle-ground solution.

The distance between viewpoints of politically well-integrated and extremely alienated citizens is nearly as great or greater on the subject of national political institutions. Asked whether the "political parties make government pay attention to what people think," more than 40 percent of the most allegiant group replied, "Yes, a good deal of attention." As Figure 4-3 points out, less than 17 percent of the most alienated citizens felt this way. Asked the same sort of question about Congress, politically well-integrated respondents were more than five times as likely as their alienated counterparts to reply that "congressmen pay a good deal of attention to what people think when making decisions." Byron, of course, has good reason to feel this way. He knows several Georgia congressmen on a first-name basis, and he's friendly with any number of state representatives. Byron is something of an exception; but Arnold gives the same response, even though he's never actually met a congressman, and the only time he's written to Washington was during the hearings on breakfast

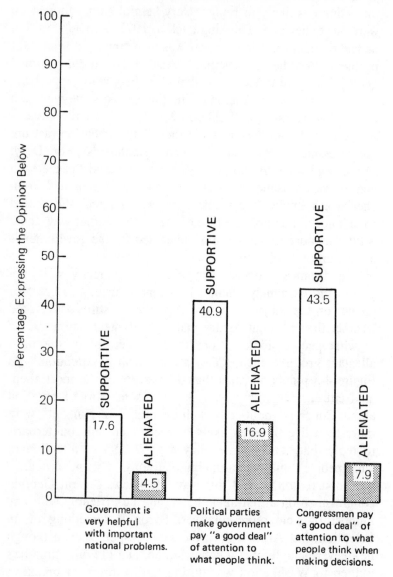

FIGURE 4-3.
Percentage of Positive Opinions about Government
by the Most Allegiant and Supportive Americans and the
Most Alienated Americans, 1972

cereal nutrition. Still, he received prompt answers to those letters, and the whole business was dropped soon afterward.
What's more, he knows "for sure" that representatives of his
company will receive a sympathetic hearing from Congress
whenever they have serious problems. For him, that's what is
most important.

Along with their belief in traditional political institutions,
governmentally supportive citizens are much more likely than
others to identify with one of the two major political parties.
Most of them, like Arnold Dryden, are Republicans. In 1972,
some 53 percent of this group said that they thought of themselves as Republicans, as compared with less than 35 percent
in the total sample of the whole population. Almost all the
rest said that they were Democrats. Byron Vining voted for
Richard Nixon in three presidential elections, yet he remains
a loyal southern Democrat in Georgia. His friends know, of
course, that if the southern trend toward Strom Thurmond
Republicanism continues,[15] and becomes stronger at the state
and local levels, Byron will probably switch parties. Despite
the national trend away from partisanship and toward independence of the political parties, only about 8 percent of the
best integrated citizens called themselves "independents" in
1972, while over 30 percent of the electorate at-large responded either that they were "independents" or that they had
no party preference. Moreover, these are the Americans, like
Arnold, who were most likly to attach bumper stickers, wear
"Nixon Now" lapel buttons, attend rallies and campaign
meetings, ring door bells, and contribute to political campaigns. They are the mainstays of traditional American political fish fries, benefit dinners, galas, and political hoopla.
A majority of this group does not attend, rally, or contribute
to be sure, but they are far more involved than national averages for all citizens. By and large, they make up the small
percentage of Americans who do become actively involved in
national politics beyond the simple fact of voting. And a ma-

jority of these politically integrated Americans told the ISR interviewers that they had tried "to influence the votes of others" during the 1972 campaign.

The men and women we have called the allegiant or well-integrated and supportive citizens number about 20 percent of the population. For 1972 this figure was smaller than the extremely alienated figure identified by our combined scale. No doubt the percentage of strong believers in governmental performance declined with the impact of Watergate. But their importance to government and their support for slow incremental change is vastly out of proportion to their numbers. Because they represent the establishment and have done so for so long, they often appear in many people's minds to represent the majority. Their numerical strength has eroded as their optimism for the American system has somewhat faded recently, but they continue to be the moneyed and most influential group in America, setting models and embodying the myths of American society—the self-made man, the vital importance of material success and "progress," and the virtue of fervent patriotism. They are likely to accept whole heartedly not only the political system but also the public and private organizations to which they have become attached.

Rachael Morrison

Rachael is a government research assistant who has recently moved to a new apartment complex in Chevy Chase, Maryland. She commutes daily to the National Security Agency nearby. She doesn't "have any real contact" in her new neighborhood, but sometimes she sees a friend or two from work in the evening or on weekends. She also dates "a guy from my old division in the Agency," but that's "only off and on and doesn't seem to be going anywhere serious. And, anyhow, he lives back in town [Washington, D.C.]." Now that Rachael is nearing thirty, she's beginning to receive anxious letters and calls from her mother in Arizona about the importance of marriage. But Rachael says her mother "is a lot more concerned about that subject" than she is.

Rachael graduated from Loyola University in 1967:

> Then I went down to "glorious" Miami to be a part of the "fabulous" singles scene down there—you know, the beach, a great tan, night life, and all that. I guess it just wasn't all that great, and everything sure was expensive. I was pretty disappointed. After studying Russian all the way through college and all that history and geography and stuff, here I was typing and filing insurance forms all day long in an office that didn't have any windows. I couldn't even look out at the palm trees, and with the kind of money they were paying, it was a joke. I could hardly even pay my rent. Then half the guys that asked me out turned out to be already married anyway. Let me tell you, I took the Civil Service Exam just as soon as it came up, and that's how I got here.

When Rachael first came to Washington, she took a small apartment in Georgetown. "But that didn't last long, because it was still awfully expensive for me, even with the better salary. And the area just really wasn't that safe." When one of her girl friends at the Agency suggested that they share one of the gleaming apartments just finished in southwest Washington, Rachael decided to try it. "It was kind of high, even with two of us, but it was really neat, and we had a great time there for almost two years." Then Rachael's roommate got married, and Rachael decided to take a less expensive apartment across the river in Arlington, Virginia. "I never really did get to know anybody out there, but it was still okay until I had a chance at a higher grade [civil service classification with higher pay] at the Agency where I am now. That meant driving all the way across town to the Maryland side every day, and it was just too much of a hassle. That's why I moved to this apartment. It has a pool and all, so it's really even better."

In between moves, Rachael has done a good deal of traveling. Twice she has driven to Arizona to see her parents, who now live in a sprawling retirement village of the "Sun City" variety. Once she and her girl friend drove to New York for a long weekend, and another time they drove together down to Miami for a week. For the past two winters she's gone to Bermuda for a week, but it was "sort of cold" each time, so next winter it will probably be the Virgin Islands or Martinique.

Rachael cares more about these tactical arrangements of life than she does about politics, but she does "try to keep up with things, because you just have to here." Still, she wishes "there weren't so much politics in government, because that would make things an awful lot easier." Rachael knows that "there are lots of problems in government, but there are always lots of problems in any large organization, and that's really what government is." As far as she's concerned, "government does the best it can," and the government employees she knows "work awfully hard and really do a good job." "Sure, there are things that are wrong; Watergate really was a mess. But it put everything out of proportion—all the good that's been done." The "real problem" with government as far as Rachael is personally concerned is "the Democrats and the Republicans," who "make up those bitter fights just out of thin air to catch the six o'clock news and score points on the agencies or the President."

Rachael knows that the government has been good to her in connection with her job. Not only does she now have an "almost ideal place to live," but she's drawing a "decent salary" that makes possible a new car, the trips she wants to take, and a lot of other things she's "always wanted to have." In the Agency, she's able to "really use a lot of that stuff I learned in college," and now the government is paying for her to continue her education at night at the School of Foreign Affairs at Georgetown University. She may even get a year off to go full-time for a master's degree—with pay. "Let me tell you, that insurance company down in Miami sure wasn't going to do that! And I didn't have anything like important work to do down there either. Here I'm really taking part in the national security. . . . I know they have to run a check on the guys I date, but that doesn't really matter."

Considering her dislike for overt partisan politics, it's not surprising that she has no strong attachment for either party. She does say, "If I have to choose, I guess I'd probably have to say that I'm a Republican, just not a very good Republican. I really think it's *the man* that makes the difference, don't you?" Rachael voted for Hubert Humphrey in 1968 and for Richard Nixon in 1972.

Citizens of the Nation

Rachael Morrison, along with Arnold and Emily Dryden, ranks among the millions who represent the new American social life. They are highly mobile—moving from one virtually indistinguishable suburban enclave or guarded urban apartment building to another, barely noticing the changing state lines and political jurisdictions. They are truly citizens of the nation and transients in any one locale. Rachael has been in her new place for several months now, but she doesn't yet "know what they do for a government out here. Frankly, it doesn't really seem very important." Arnold and Emily have children, and they're somewhat more concerned about local services, particularly the schools. Arnold and other corporate-oriented respondents told us, however, that they "just didn't have time" to worry about local politics or to become active.

Analysis of the 1972 election data shows that Americans who had lived in their communities only a relatively short while (less than six months) were no more alienated from politics than those who had lived in the same community all their lives. This is a striking finding. Ordinarily, one would expect that dislocation and relocation would be crucial to political estrangement. The aloofness of new "neighbors" in transient communities, the commercialism of the "Welcome Wagon" after a move to a different suburb, and apartment dwellers riding the same elevator for months without developing so much as a nodding acquaintance with their neighbors should bear this out.

The mystery clears up somewhat when it is fully understood that a great many of America's perpetual "newcomers" are *corporate* men and women. Whether they live in the polished suburbs of Grand Rapids, Michigan, Boca Raton, Florida, White Plains, New York, San Diego, California, or Chevy Chase, Maryland, they are almost inevitably associated with General Foods, IBM, the military-security establishment, or the like. Each is a well-paid cog in a national or international organization, a professional network, or both. The obvious social isolation and "anomie" of geographic rootlessness is evidently offset by the economic rewards of corporate success.[16] "All the moving around is okay," one corporate housewife declared, "so long as we're moving up."

Most of the men and women in the large private and public bureaucracies are indeed moving to move up. Arnold has become a latter-day nomad, buying and selling his houses and moving his entire family back and forth across the country for the sake of the company, to be sure, but also for the benefit of his own career progress. More recently Arnold has been on the move by plane from his newest home base in Michigan, spanning the continent for meetings and one-night stands from Los Angeles to New York and back again. This is all part of the process of "moving up" from his already advanced level.

Since Rachael entered government service, her residential moving has been confined to the Washington, D.C., area, but if the opportunity arises, no doubt she will move farther. She is now quite committed to the life she leads and the benefits and pay she receives. And after all, only about 11 percent of all federal employees actually work in the Washington area. For Rachael, a move to a similar apartment in "a safe area" near New York, San Francisco, or Chicago would entail little more disorientation than her present transition from Arlington to Chevy Chase.[17]

Aside from moving, other aspects of social isolation such as noninvolvement with group life, the lack of friendships and other human contacts still appear related to political estrangement.[18] Nonetheless, corporate Americans seem, for the most part, to have overcome the social isolation that would logically go along with rootlessness and itinerancy. Their associations and human involvements are largely structured for them by the national or international organizations for which they work.

Aaron Rouse

Occupationally, Americans with strongest allegiance to the national political system have been craftsmen and foremen. Their allegiance to the system, in percentage terms, has been even greater than that of the large-corporate and small-business managers and professionals. One of these independent craftsmen is Aaron Rouse, a mason and contractor operating out of Argyle, New York. Until recently, Aaron was one of the strongest supporters of American politics-as-usual. He still has firm views about citizen responsibilities:

> I gave the three best years of my life for freedom in this
> country, and I don't want to see it given away now. Half
> the people around here don't even bother to vote, and a lot
> of those that do will vote in just about any fool project

89

that's on the ballot. You think they care how much it costs?
Why, no, they're not goin' to pay nothin'. They're drawin'
welfare.

Now they want to put zoning in around here, tell a man
where he can build his house and where he can't. I believe
that if a man's got some land he ought to be able to do
what he wants with it.

There was a time, not long ago, when Aaron's personal
code also included uncritical loyalty to national leaders. When
the Nixon administration first came under attack because of
the Watergate scandal, Aaron was incensed at the repeated
criticism and press coverage. "They ought to just leave him
[Nixon] alone," he said during the winter of 1973. "They can't
prove anything on him anyway." But as the magnitude of
proof accumulated over months of evidence gathering, hearings, and new revelations, Aaron's loyalty waned. His general
feeling of cynicism and political distrust soared:

Anyone who's in office has gotta go. Clean them all out
is what I say. Let them know we don't have to put up with
this kind of business. It doesn't matter what party they're in.
If they're in there now, I'm voting against them.

I used to think it was just the press stirring up all this
trouble, but not anymore. These politicians we've got just
can't say anything but lies—like that story about an
accidental eighteen-minute gap in Nixon's tape. I may be
stupid, but I'm not that stupid!

Aaron's rising disillusionment with national politics has also
heightened his awareness and intolerance of the government
regulations and red tape that affect his work:

They've got inspectors comin' around every two minutes
fining me if one of the men doesn't have on his hardhat.
Why, it's crazy! Nobody'll be workin' above ground level,
and it's 95 degrees in the shade. I can't make the men
keep on those hats under those conditions. Now they're
enforcing a new one, making us keep our electric lines up

on poles. You can't believe how much time and trouble
that's causing us. And for what? . . . I can't even remember
all the forms and papers I've gotta fill out now. Don't half
of 'em amount to anything, but you can believe I've gotta
do them. This stuff has just gotta stop so we can get back
on a more realistic basis. Otherwise, I just don't see how
anyone's gonna be able to build anything anymore.

As this book is written, conclusive data on the nationally
heightened sense of political alienation in the aftermath of
Watergate have yet to be reported. But it is clear that Aaron
is not alone in his change of attitude. For many Americans,
feelings of firm allegiance to their national government have
turned to disillusionment and suspicion. Louis Harris reported,
for example, that the 46 percent who agreed in 1967 that
"most politicians are in politics to make money for themselves" had expanded to 63 percent by late 1973.[19] Even
before the scandals of the 1970s emerged, the political allegiance of men like Aaron Rouse was in measurable decline.

chapter 5

The Apathetic Americans

Martha Harris

Martha Harris guesses she's "never been much interested in politics." She's "thought about votin' sometimes; I know I oughta. But with the children an' all, an' specially little David, I just can't seem to get down to the right office in town. I think you have to get registration papers an' all, an' it's awful hard for me." Martha isn't strongly alienated from American politics. In fact, she imagines that "they's prob'ly some pretty good men up there. . . . Oh, they's gonna be a few bad apples, but I guess they's mostly all right." By and large, Martha is simply *indifferent* to politics.[1] She hasn't thought much about the candidates or political parties in any given election. When asked whether political leaders in Washington care about what people like her think, she says she hopes they do, "but sometimes I think they just don't care about us at all. . . . I just don't know. I let my husband take care of all that. He's the one that votes in the family. You should be talkin' to him."

Martha doesn't do many of the things that active people do without so much as a second thought. But with five children, the youngest of them retarded, and no car, the costs of time, transportation, and child care have been too high for her. Instead of worrying about the possibility of voting she's content to just "forget about it" or relegate the responsibility to her husband.

Martha grew up in Tulsa, Oklahoma, where she "spent a lot of time at the doctor's because of my hormone problem." Evidentaly that didn't help, and it appears that her obesity will be a life-long difficulty. Martha's parents have worked for many years in a small but highly popular diner. She also worked there for a time. She still vividly remembers the troubles she had: "The owner kept gettin' on me for droppin' things, an' I got awful nervous. I kept burnin' myself awful, an' after awhile he said he didn't want me workin' anymore until I could learn to look after myself better. But he gave me another chance 'cause my folks really needed the money. That time I did real good; never got burnt again and never dropped more than two plates in the next three years."

Martha's parents still work at the same diner, know everybody, and feel it's "home." Although they're getting older, once a year they make the car trip down to Texas to see their grandchildren. Martha has never been back.

Almost twenty years ago, Martha's husband, Ben, was sent by his company to Tulsa for "a few weeks" on an installation job. The company was the largest manufacturer of industrial boilers in the Southwest. "Well, that few weeks was longer than anybody'd figured, an' he just kept eatin' in the diner an' seein' me nights," Martha recalls. "After four months, Ben was ready to go back to Dallas, an' we got married an' left together. After awhile, we were able to get this place out here in Grand Prairie. Oh, but how it's growed since then."

The company has also grown a lot since then, at least it did until last year when it was purchased by a conglomerate. Ben has stayed on as a repair and installation man, still traveling a good deal while Martha stays home with the children. "Watchin' the children takes up most all my time, and little

David just can't be left alone, even with Nona [her oldest]. I have to take him with me most places so's he don't do no damage to hisself or the house." As far as Martha is concerned, this is her "job," and the house is her "place." Relations with the external world, paying taxes and bills, keeping track of the insurance and bank loans, are beyond her. As with voting, these areas are left to Ben. "He takes care of all that."

The Apathetic Response

Apathetic Americans like Martha Harris offer a contrast to the Byron Vinings, Arnold Drydens, and Rachael Morrisons. Those who are most in tune with the economic, organizational, and political systems usually care quite a lot about their political beliefs as well as their jobs and material successes. Apathetic Americans ordinarily do not have as large a stake in the organizational world, and politics is their last concern. Their response is one of indifference to politics and normally noninvolvement or withdrawal from political participation. In 1972 they were only about half as likely to have voted in the presidential election as those who expressed interest in American politics.[2] And in that year less than 12 percent of the apathetic attempted to influence the vote of others, compared with 44 percent of their politically interested counterparts.

An apathetic person like Martha normally doesn't have the political knowledge or the alienated focus of Jenny Jackson in her squalid Newark flat or Joyce White in Louisville. Jenny and Joyce know that they have been let down by the government, that their hopes have been frustrated, and that political officials are "just in it to get rich." They have lost interest in politics and, for the time being, have withdrawn, whereas Martha never had an interest to begin with and never was involved.[3]

The Americans who "don't care much" about politics make

up a sizeable minority of the population, about 24 percent in 1972. Like other minority groups, they have been subject to a good deal of name calling: "slackers," "idiots," and the "deadwood of democracy," among others.[4] It is often assumed that they are the nonvoters in elections and are probably alienated as well. E. E. Schattschneider calls them "the soft underbelly of the system." In Schattschneider's view, they are the "least involved or most convinced that the system is loaded against" them and "the most likely point of subversion." He concludes, "This is the *sickness* of democracy."[5] Seymour Martin Lipset argues that political apathy is neither good nor bad for democracy: "It is only when a major crisis or effective authoritarian movement suddenly pulls the normally disaffected into the political area that the system is threatened."[6] Heinz Eulau takes the salutory tack that nonvoting is a manifestation of "the politics of happiness." Americans are reasonably content with the way things are going so they just don't bother to become involved.[7] It all sounds plausible, and no one has been much fettered by firm data one way or another.

The place to begin an assessment of such arguments and to gain a better grasp of the apathetic response to politics is with an understanding of what is meant by the term "apathetic." Like alienation, the idea of political apathy has been overworked. Most commonly, the term has been confused with estrangement from politics and with nonvoting.[8] In our view, the apathetic "response" is essentially a nonresponse to politics, the disinterested shrug of "I don't care much" and "I don't pay much attention" to government elections and public affairs.

A number of questions in the national surveys touched on this feeling, but there were three questions that consistently formed a cumulative scale of political apathy.* They are the following:

* The responses, scoring, and Guttman Scale characteristics of these questions may be found in the appendix.

> Generally speaking, would you say that you personally care a good deal which party wins the presidential election this fall, or that you don't care much which party wins?

> Some people don't pay much attention to the political campaigns. How about you, would you say that you have been very much interested, somewhat interested, or not much interested in following the political campaigns so far this year?

> Some people seem to follow what's going on in government and public affairs most of the time whether there's an election going on or not. Others aren't that interested. Would you say you follow what's going on in government and public affairs most of the time, some of the time, only now and then, or hardly at all?

Since 1960, which is as far back as these particular questions were uniformly asked, roughly 10 percent of the national cross section answered all three questions with an uninterested or uncaring response. About 25 percent consistently gave apathetic answers to at least two of these questions. In Figure 5-1 both of these response patterns show up as nearly parallel and relatively flat lines. Superimposed across these lines is a third line showing the striking increase in the number of politically alienated Americans who are interested in national elections and public affairs, not apathetic about them.

Apathy, then, says nothing about one's views of government and politics; it's simply a matter of political interest. As it turns out, many of the most alienated citizens are uninterested as well, about 44 percent in 1972. But nearly 56 percent of the alienated Americans express concern about election outcomes and public affairs.[9] In other words, there is a relationship between alienation and apathy, but they are by no means the same thing.

Not surprisingly, a majority of apathetic Americans, like Martha, admit that they did not vote in 1972. In contrast, nearly 69 percent of the interested but extremely alienated

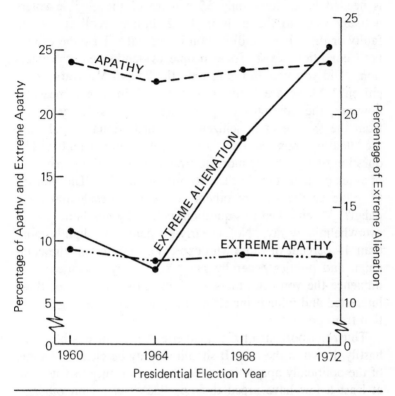

FIGURE 5-1.
Percentage of Political Apathy[a] and Extreme Apathy[b]
by Percentage of Extreme Alienation, 1960-1972

[a]Respondents were termed "apathetic" if they answered two of the three scaled apathy questions with responses indicating political disinterest.

[b]"Extreme apathy" denotes those respondents who answered all three of the scaled apathy questions indicating their lack of interest in politics.

citizens say that they did vote in 1972. But a word of caution is needed here. Since only 55 percent of the eligible voters actually went to the polls in 1972, either recollections are faulty or there is some distortion in the data. To some extent, both conditions exist. Some people evidently hear the question, "Did you vote in the last election?" as "Are you a good citizen?" Many are loath to say, "No." In larger measure, however, the difference in percentages reflects the exclusion from the sample of noncitizens, the institutional population, the "floating" population, and the mental incompetents.[10] The question that probably more accurately reflects the percentage of voter participation in the citizenry at large is, "Did you try to influence the vote of others during the presidential campaign?" When asked this question, politically apathetic people overwhelmingly say, "No" (nearly 90 percent). Slightly more than 44 percent of those who express an interest in the campaign and politics generally say, "Yes," they did attempt to influence the votes of others. Curiously, over a third of these interested and influencing citizens also expressed strong alienation from politics.[11]

Thus, the portrait of the apathetic American has been too hastily drawn in the past. It should already be clear that some of the politically apathetic do feel a sense of duty to vote, and at least a few have urged their particular views on others.[12] As we shall see, these are people who respond in different ways to American politics.

Willy O'Reilly

Willy is the janitor of an elementary school in northern New Jersey. He doesn't like his work. "The pay isn't half as good as welfare, and the kids do just about everything they can think of to make my job as miserable as possible. Last week they stopped up every damn toilet in the school, damned near burnt the place down settin' a fire in a trash can, and took the library door off its hinges. An' you should see the stuff they throw away: good paper, art supplies, erasers—I'm goin' straight to the school board about it, I'm tellin' you."

Willy's words for national political leaders aren't any kinder: "They're the biggest bunch of no good bums God ever let live! Isn't one of 'em since Kennedy 'at was good 'nough to run for dog catcher. Look at that Nixon! There isn't a bigger crook anywhere! An' the rest of 'em's just about as bad; just give 'em the chance. Who was that other fella? I must of voted for him; always do; always vote for the one that ain't had his chance to steal yet. Might as well give 'em all a chance to steal my money. Why, I'm givin' welfare to the politicians!"

It may seem curious that Willy bothers to vote. He has no faith in the party system; he's distrustful in the extreme; and he knows full well that "they don't give a damn what the workin' man thinks." Willy doesn't really care who wins an election, presidential or otherwise. As long as he gets a chance to vote against the incumbent, he has accomplished his political mission. There are occasions when he does attend local public meetings to point an accusing finger at the school children, at members of the school board, or at both. That makes him something of a local character, and apparently he enjoys that distinction. But as for following national affairs: "I don't even read the papers anymore, and those jerks on TV make me wanna throw up. It's always the same, ya steal enough an' y're a 'statesman.' "

Willy may be a bit more outspoken and colorful than others who are *disgruntled* about national and local political life, but the thrust of his comments and his continued interest in voting are characteristic of about 19 percent of those who are politically apthetic. This is clearly not "the politics of happiness" or the "soft underbelly" of anything. Willy and others are the chronically resentful citizens who are convinced that the system is loaded against them. They don't really care to follow the system's progress, but as long as they have the opportunity, they will vote, usually against an incumbent (see note 12).

Wanda Knutsen

We met Wanda Knutsen standing in line at a snack bar near Jones Beach, Long Island. It was her day off, and she and her boyfriend, Carl, had come out from Queens for a day of surfing. "But the waves aren't any good," Carl said. "It's too flat." They had time to talk while waiting for a breeze to come up.

Wanda works as a cashier in one of the discount drug stores in her neighborhood. "It's boring sometimes," Wanda says, "but the pay is pretty good now that we have the union. Besides, it's not half as boring as school, and now I have the money to do what I want afterwards." Wanda left school after tenth grade, and she's been working ever since. That was four years ago. Now she has her own efficiency apartment, and evidently she spends a lot of time enjoying life. "We love to take rides, specially here to the beach. Last week we went to the races at Belmont. 'Course, it was awful during the gas shortage, but there's always something—the movies, TV, always something."

Politics simply isn't a part of Wanda's world. She was perplexed by our questionnaire: "So many questions! Is anybody really interested in all that stuff?" We assured her that some were. Wanda wasn't. She has never registered to vote and just doesn't "think about that at all." Asked if she thought she might vote in the next presidential election, she said, "Oh, I don't know. So many millions of people vote. My vote just wouldn't make any difference. I guess I just don't have any interest in those things." [13] Carl, who says he's not much interested either, helped her out a bit: "That just isn't one of our big topics." Even so, Wanda is not estranged from national

100

political leaders: "Yes, I think they try to represent all the people, and they do a good job too, I guess. Well, I do worry about the prices going up all the time. We have to change them all the time in the drug store . . . but I think they're doing the best they can." Wanda feels that there are "probably" differences between the two political parties, and even after the worst revelations of Watergate, she was sure that "most" of the men in national government were still honest.

In a word, Wanda is *content* with the way national political life is going without her interest or participation. Wanda does seem to fit the mold of "the politics of happiness." But she and others like her constitute only about 4 percent of the apathetic Americans, and that is only about 1 percent of the total population with voting potential.[14] This means simply that people like Wanda are difficult to locate in the American electorate, and the notion of many contented Wanda's forming the basis of an American "politics of happiness" might best be forgotten. Most apathetic people are more like Martha Harris or Wanda's boyfriend, Carl. While they may be somewhat cynical about the words and actions of politicians, they may no longer see any important meaning in the party system, or they may be generally disillusioned to some degree, they are not as content with politics as is Wanda or as extremely alienated from politics as is Willy O'Reilly.

Sharon McRae

Sharon McRae is beautiful. Her hair is long and blond, and at twenty-one her skin has a clear glow. She wears the same faded denim jacket and dungarees to her college classes each week, always clean but always the same. Sharon says that the biggest problem in America is materialism. She's the voice of youthful idealism left over for the seventies.

Sharon grew up on the outskirts of Providence, Rhode Island, and describes herself as "a hippy" in the context of her suburban high school there. At that time she was "very active in the students' rights movement and in antiwar stuff," which was then the vogue in colleges and in some high schools. "I'm glad I was, because I got that out of my system before college. In fact, that's what I learned in high school." With bus loads of others, she went to Washington, demonstrated, petitioned, and came home to demonstrate some more in her home town and to write to congressmen. "We ran up against the fact that as students we had no rights. We couldn't pass out pamphlets at school or circulate petitions or do anything political there. So we contacted the ACLU and almost had a test case. But we kind of wore out after awhile, and we never went to court, and never had the test case."

The group Sharon worked with did attempt to start an alternative high school in the area, and that effort met with greater success than the national thrust. Such a school was actually established the year after she graduated. The very word graduation stirs a gleeful gleam: "The principal who had been there for about fifty years retired the year after I graduated. We had the feeling that after us he needed to retire. (No, don't put that down.) But I wore out too. It's like beating your head against a stone wall."

After high school, Sharon went to a small experimental college in northern New England, but she dropped out before the end of her first term. "That was the most apathetic place in the world. We couldn't even get up a bus load of kids to go down and protest the Cambodian invasion. They just wanted to sit around and smoke dope. It was absurd."

Sharon worked at a number of places after this dry-run at college: the campus snack bar, a bakery, a health food store, a natural foods restaurant. Then a friend who was involved with "the prisoners' rights movement" talked her into a visit to the state penitentiary in a nearby town. "I said, 'Okay, sure I'll go.' It was just a lark." This "lark" became, for Sharon, a moving experience that ripened into single-minded commitment. A month later, after visiting inmates two or

102

three times a week, she moved in with the wife of a prisoner to become involved full time with the prison community. Six months later, she decided to reenter college, this time at the nearest state college, in the "criminal justice" program.

Sharon is outraged by what she has seen of the prison world:

They more or less rot while they're there. Talk about rehabilitation, they don't even know the word at that place. There's hardly a one of them that doesn't come out worse, debilitated by the experience. I could tell you stories that would . . . How did I work with the prisoners? It was easy, I was so damn mad! I think it was Pound who said, "When the punishment evokes more honest horror than the crime, the law is wrong." Well, that's just how I felt.

But mostly I just educated myself, talked with the prisoners, talked with wardens, and prisoners' wives. Then one day a prisoner sat me down and told me I wasn't going to get anywhere, that I'd have to get a real education before I could do anything at all about the way I felt. That's why I'm here in this program.

Sharon doesn't sound apathetic; she certainly isn't like Martha or Wanda. But on the national level, she "could care less":

Oh, I might make the effort to vote against a type like Nixon if I had the chance, he was such a Goddamned criminal. But it really doesn't make any difference. They're all so corrupt, and there just isn't anything we can do to stop them. Washington politics is so big, so far out there, I just can't relate. I don't even read about it anymore.

Sharon's antipathy for national policy and politics is now compounded by disinterest. She has tuned out, retreated to local concerns and *withdrawn*.

Political Withdrawal

Sharon McRae is nearly the archetypal student activist turned "dropout" during the late 1960s and early 1970s.

These were the young people given so much attention and prominence by the "youth cult" writers and media managers of the time. The "flower children" who tuned in to Timothy Leary's and Ken Kesey's messages about the possibilities of "innerspace" travel with drugs,[15] the hordes of peaceful thousands thronging to Woodstock Nation, and the youthful "revolutionaries" on dozens of college campuses flinging the rhetoric of radical political change at nightly TV audiences— all of these indicated to many observers that the times were "a changin'." Others thought that they saw the shape of the future in these stylistic expressions. Theodore Roszak, for example, explains these youthful styles and outbursts as inescapable reactions to a faceless technocracy: "So, by way of a dialectic Marx could never have imagined, technocratic Ameria produces a potentially revolutionary element among its own youth. The bourgeoisie, instead of discovering the class enemy in its factories, finds it across the breakfast table in the person of its own pampered young."[16] The developments of the late 1960s make it clear, Roszak concludes, "that the generational revolt is not likely to pass over in a few years' time. The ethos of disaffiliation is still in the process of broadening down through the adolescent years, picking up numbers as time goes on."[17]

Observing the same events and expressions, Yale Law Professor Charles Reich became so enthusiastic about the possibilities of the new youth consciousness that he eloquently urged corporate professionals and other bureaucrats to emulate their juniors, to loosen their ties and styles, to climb fewer mountains more slowly, and to become more involved with their natural and human surroundings. All this would come anyway, because as Reich predicts:

> There is a revolution coming. It will not be like revolutions of the past. It will originate with the individual and with culture, and it will change the political structure only as its final act. . . .

This is the revolution of the new generation. Their protest
and rebellion, their culture, clothes, music, drugs, ways
of thought, and liberated life style are not a passing fad or a
form of dissent and refusal, nor are they in any sense
irrational. The whole emerging pattern, from ideals to
campus demonstrations to beads and bell bottoms to the
Woodstock Festival, makes sense and is a part of a
consistent philosophy. It is both necessary and inevitable,
and in time it will include not only youth but all people in
America.[18]

In Reich's view, this revolution of youth, or "Consciousness
III," would take place because the American "Corporate
State," would "self-destruct" as the cooperation of heretofore
willing workers and consumers ended.

Other observers took a much less sanguine view of the
youth culture as a means of "greening" the American future.
Malcolm Muggeridge termed Reich's future view "unresisting
imbecility," wondering in print, "How a population stupefied
with pot, allergic to any form of discipline or self-control,
nomadic, promiscuous and indulgent is to keep the dark
satanic mills of technology going." [19] Stewart Alsop character-
ized the youth cult phenomenon as a profoundly antiintellec-
tual "bag of scary mush" that incarnated dark visions of
fascism and memories of what Adolph Hitler called "my in-
tuition." [20]

Whatever the merits of these particular visions and por-
trayals, the question that fairly begs to be answered is, after
the passage of several years, does the cause of all this concern
and debate still exist? Signs and symbols of the Consciousness
III that Reich described are still visible among the young
people on college campuses, at the country craft shows, and
on the interstate highway interchanges, but statistically, as
the 1970s mature, the answer appears to be, "No." Analysis of
the 1972 election survey shows no relationship between a
person's age and political apathy. Young people under thirty

are, if anything, less likely to be apathetic—to dropout politically—than are their elders. Among the young, those who are still students and those who have had college training are the least apathetic of all in terms of population percentages. Youthful disinterest in "the system" simply has not accelerated in the way many had projected or feared as the decade began. However, on an impressionistic level, it appears that student apathy toward the society as a whole has, in fact, declined. Colleagues across the country lament or are elated about the return to the 1950s. Even the vacuous songs have come back into vogue, and "grade grubbing" has returned to the campuses along with the Marine Corps recruiters. The Central Intelligence Agency and the U.S. Foreign Service report swollen lists of high-quality applicants.

Those who have withdrawn from American politics, who have become so alienated from and disinterested in governmental affairs that they have ceased to participate, are most typically not the disaffected student demonstrators and dropouts who gained so much notoriety a few years ago. Numerically they are likely to be the men and women, more often the women, of any age who are lowest on the social and economic ladders. More than a third of the apathetic Americans are found in the lowest income category, coming from families that earned less than $4,000 in 1972. Almost two-thirds of these apathetic people are from families that earned less than $6,000 in 1972.[21] In the era of high material expectations thwarted by even higher inflation, the disenchantment and withdrawal of Americans at these levels of income is probably not surprising. A low level of formal education intensifies this effect. Of those found in the lowest two income categories and who dropped out before completing high school, 40 percent expressed apathy toward American politics.[22] These were also the people who were least likely to vote in elections or otherwise to participate politically.

The surveys studied did not interview the same people between 1960 and 1972, so we cannot account for certain changes. It would be fascinating to know, for example, how many people, like Sharon, became disillusioned with the national government and then frustrated by the futility of political participation to the point that they drifted into apathy and nonparticipation. Perhaps there are more people like Martha who were never interested in politics and who gradually lost their faith and allegiance to American government because of the impacts of the past decade. Unfortunately, the order in which people arrive at these feelings cannot be gleaned from the data. We do know, however, that about 40 percent of all alienated Americans were found in the "withdrawn" group—apathetic and nonparticipating—in 1972. We also know that as political alienation has steadily increased in America, proportionately fewer alienated citizens are also apathetic. Unlike Sharon, many of these alienated people are not only still concerned about national politics but they are also still actively involved.

The Abstainers

Alan and Jean Arthur read the *Los Angeles Times* daily as well as the local San Diego paper. They rarely miss the evening TV news. As an accountant, Alan can hardly afford to be behind on national events, and Jean has a healthy interest of her own. But the Arthurs didn't vote in 1972. Alan felt that McGovern was "a lightweight" who represented only a "fringe" of the Democratic party and "just couldn't handle" the kinds of problems now facing the country. He viewed Nixon as "a political eel." "Anyone halfway alert knew he was a crooked SOB twenty years ago." Jean admits that she's influenced by her husband's thinking on politics but says, "I felt the same way myself. I honestly didn't see how I could vote for either one of them."

Up in Maine, Tricia Woods voted for George McGovern.

107

She knew it "wouldn't do any good, but what the hell." Sherman Woods left the presidential columns blank. "It didn't make any difference," he said. "McGovern wasn't gonna make it, an' Nixon is just another capitalist rip-off."

Jenny Jackson in Newark hasn't withdrawn from politics either. She is thoroughly disillusioned and very much disheartened about her future prospects, but she is still "keepin' up on things." Yet she didn't see any point in voting in 1972. "Nixon wasn't gonna do nothin' for us, an' that other fella wasn't gonna win. What good was that? They ain't none of 'em care about us anyhow."

John Shearworth wanted to write in a vote for George Wallace, even after Wallace had been shot down and paralyzed. John *"knew* Bremmer didn't act alone" and that "they wanted to *get* the one candidate who had really mattered." John wanted to "show them" anyway, but when election day came, he didn't go to the polls. He knew it wouldn't count, and there was no one else he wanted to vote for. He abstained.

Alan and Jean, Sherman, Jenny, and John are among the many abstainers in the American political system. They are not apathetic about what goes on politically; they can hardly afford to be. But for now they don't vote, they don't attempt to influence others, they don't attend political meetings, and they don't contribute to political campaigns. They see no point in it. In a country where almost 45 percent of the eligible electorate refrained from voting in the last major election, this is a powerful latent force for change. In 1972, using the citizen's attempt to influence the votes of others as an indicator of political participation, it may be shown that over 65 percent of those interested but alienated people abstained from political participation.[23]

The alienated but attentive nonvoter may be drawn back into the political system at any time, and probably more readily than those who have ceased to care. When a candidate of honesty and evident political strength appears, when it seems as if he might have a chance against an entrenched establishment, when it appears that he may truly deliver for black people, and when, most importantly, the new candidate has issues that touch realistically on their lives, there is little doubt that Alan and Jean, Sherman, Jenny, and John will be back in the polling booths.

The Reformers

In Gary, Indiana, Ward Beloit is an active voter who hopes that a candidate in the traditional Democratic Party will "bring the situation back under control." He's rather sure that "a firm hand" will be necessary, but he doesn't yet know what that might entail. Still, "something's got to be done," in his view, to stem the tide of inflation and scarcity. "I'm getting farther and farther behind both with wages at the mill and also in my farming operation. It doesn't seem like any of these politicians have cared at all about the guy who's trying to make an honest living."

Thoroughly disgusted with the Vietnam war in November, 1968, Deryl Minter left his downtown law practice early so that he could be back in Westchester well before the polls closed. He voted for comedian Dick Gregory. A number of his friends were abstaining entirely, but he wanted to put in "some kind of a protest vote." Otherwise he couldn't see any significant difference between the two major candidates, Humphrey and Nixon, except, as he now puts it, "Nixon turned out to be even more incredible than we had always thought." In 1972 both he and his wife, Sandra, voted for George McGovern.

Judith Weissman voted in 1972, largely because, as a citizen, "that's what you're supposed to do." But in her area of exurban Portland, not many other people favored George McGovern. Judith believes in what McGovern stood for, but she thought he "fell apart" during the campaign. "That [Sen-

109

ator Thomas] Eagleton business was just awful," she declared.
"I believed in a lot of what he was saying, but it just didn't
come across as if he knew what he was talking about. Still, he
was a whole lot better than Nixon. But honestly, I don't know
if he would have made all that much difference."

About 35 percent of the most alienated Americans who retain an interest in politics continue to vote and try to influence
others. They are the reformers who hope that the government
will return to its fundamental principles and that its politics
and programs will again be based on morality. The following
chapter will show, in detail, that the alienated reformers are
often well to the left or right of center in American political
thinking. Their thoughts and candidate preferences are not
likely to be the bland, traditional ones of the well-heralded
"mainstream."

Like John Shearworth, Kentucky-based Ralph White had
also been a committed Wallace supporter in 1968. Ralph had
just begun "driving truck" at that point, and he felt strongly
about "bein' 'way from home more'n half the time, doin' this
kinda work while all those long-haired weirdos are off doin'
just 'bout anything they want—on my hard-earned money."
But by 1972 both Ralph and his wife, Joyce, had withdrawn
from American politics and didn't any longer want to hear
about politicians and political campaigns. Ralph and Joyce
had tuned out. But the Whites, especially Ralph, had been
interested in politics once, and as we shall see, people who
have withdrawn or temporarily abstained from politics may
well become involved again under the right conditions and
when a candidate or issue touches them directly.

FIGURE 5-2.
Apathetic and Alienated Americans and Their
Participation in Politics, 1972[a]

INDIFFERENT	CONTENTED	DISGRUNTLED
Apathetic Disillusioned	Apathetic Allegiant	Apathetic Alienated or Disillusioned
Nonparticipant	Nonparticipant	Participant
46% of Apathetic Citizens	4.4% of Apathetic Citizens	11% of Apathetic Citizens
MARTHA HARRIS	WANDA KNUTSEN	WILLY O'REILLY
WITHDRAWN	ABSTAINERS	REFORMERS
Apathetic Alienated Nonparticipant	Interested Alienated Nonparticipant	Interested Alienated Participant
39% of Apathetic Citizens	66% of Alienated Citizens	34% of Alienated Citizens
SHARON McRAE THE WHITES	THE ARTHURS SHERMAN WOODS JENNY JACKSON JOHN SHEARWORTH	WARD BELOIT THE MINTERS JUDITH WEISSMAN

[a]Percentages based on responses to the 1972 survey question: "Did you talk to any people and try to show them why they should vote for one of the parties or candidates?"

chapter 6
Alienation and Political Action

JUST TEN DAYS before Christmas, 1973, Ralph White pulled his twin-screw container truck into line behind twenty other trucks that were blocking the Ohio Turnpike. Ralph remembers how casually the truck-in was set up: "It was figured out that same morning. A lot of the men had been talkin' about it for days, and the ones in Pennsylvania were all over the radio. I pulled in for a stop at Zanesville around seven, and a bunch of the drivers already had it pretty well worked out. There wasn't much of anything to it, mainly just deciding where to stop." Ralph picked up his ticket at the toll gate in a long line of other trucks. "The little fat guy there knew what was goin' on, but he just kept smilin' and handin' out the tickets. He didn't give a damn." Ralph also recalls his initial nervousness. This was the first time his political actions had ever been on the line, and it was his own truck, his and the bank's, that might be fined, confiscated, or damaged.

When the Ohio State Police and the TV crews came up, all nervousness seemed to vanish. "I guess I was too close up to it to be scared anymore. It was kinda like that in Korea." A driver from one of the lead trucks stepped right up to the microphone as a camera started clicking: "Yeah, this is a protest," he said. "It's a TRUCK-IN! . . . This whole busi-

112

ness of a gas crisis is a fake. The government is pulling a fast one on us. They knew this was coming all along, and they didn't do a damn thing about it. The whole thing is just an excuse so that the big oil companies can get their prices right up where they want them. They're not going to get away with it if we have to shut down every road in the country."

Ralph remembers almost word for word what was said because he heard the statement repeated twice that night on television. In fact, television is the crucial tool in the development and success of these tactics. At about the same time, another protesting trucker stressed the importance of the medium this way, "We want Nixon and his people, when they turn on their television sets, to hear us." [1] As Ralph sees it, "It was just like George Wallace used to say, 'Send them a message up there in Washington!' We were just sending them a message."

The Milieu of Dissent

This type of political participation was as new to Ralph as it was to his fellow truckers. Ralph hadn't actually considered the "truck-in" as something "political." He had always been annoyed and angered by civil rights demonstrators, welfare strikers, and student rioters. As far as he was concerned, they were all "a bunch of lazy bums, livin' off welfare, foodstamps, and my taxes. This [truck-in] was different." For Ralph and Joyce White this political protest was indeed different. The surging prices of diesel fuel during the winter of 1973–1974 directly threatened their livelihood. As the Whites saw it, these were men trying to make a living, not just hippies or welfare cheaters.

This protest was also different because the stimulus that touched it off brought Ralph and Joyce back into the political arena. Instead of acting in the voting booth, Ralph's politics took place on the public highway, contrary to law. In this respect, the truck-in was no different than the hundreds of other protests that have filled nightly television screens for nearly two decades. Viewers have become so accustomed to political protests, including those involving considerable violence, that their shock value has long been lost.

Unless there is a call to action that is meaningful to alienated Americans, political withdrawal, abstinence, or marginal participation is their predictable response. As we have already seen, the citizens who have temporarily withdrawn or refused to take part in politics-as-usual make up a significant proportion of the nonvoting statistics. Lengthy discussions with many of them reinforced our sense that these are semidesperate people whose feelings of political impotence, suspicion, and garrulous disinterest in politics are intensified by the traditional candidates and issues presented them. From their perspective, the system has not only denied them a meaningful voice, but it has victimized them by demanding their continued payment of steadily increasing taxes to support wars or "lazy bums" they don't care for; requiring their obedience to unequally enforced rules, regulations, and laws; and commanding obeisance to performance records, SAT scores, and bureaucratic form-filling and regimentation. Yet when the opportunity presents itself—the meaningful candidate or the urgent issue—these alienated and often politically dormant Americans may be aroused. Like Ralph White, they may even be somewhat surprised by their own actions. In a political milieu of dissent and upheaval, however, demands of the alienated may be extreme and violent as well.

The postwar decades have been years of severe shocks and discontinuities. This was the era of "brinksmanship," of "nuclear parity," of "eyeball-to-eyeball diplomacy," of "fallout shelters," and Dr. Strangelove worries about whose finger was on the red button. In part these were fantasies, but they were widely held ones backed up by awesome realities.[2] Televised carnage, human torture, and the searing destruction of "liberated" villages in Southeast Asia were echoed repeatedly at home in ghetto flames, looting, ethnic gangs, mass murders, snipers, hijackings, skyjackings, kidnappings, the casual destruction of private property, and generally soaring rates of drug addiction and street crime. From the Cuban missile crisis to John Kennedy's assassination, from the burned buses of the "freedom rides" to the bloody riots in Watts, Newark, Detroit, and Washington, and the murders of Malcolm X, Medgar Evers, Martin Luther King, and Robert Kennedy, fear and violence rocked the norms of American politics. Student protesters, angry young blacks, antiwar demonstrators, as well as construction workers and truckers, had the specters of dramatic confrontation and sudden death as their everyday models for political action.

The Growing Approval of Protest

The public's acceptance and even approval of legal protest meetings and mass marches to make a political point was considerably greater in 1972 than it was just four years earlier. In 1968, protests usually meant civil rights and antiwar demonstrations. Figure 6-1 shows that in 1968 about a third of the most alienated citizens approved such action. In 1972 nearly 60 percent of the politically estranged Americans and fully 64 percent of the most allegiant citizens said that they would approve legal protest meetings and marches. As Judith Weissman sees it, "That's just about the only way you can get anyone's attention anymore."

The rising public approval of civil disobedience is even more dramatic. Figure 6-2 shows that in 1968 substantially less than a majority voiced approval. In 1972, well over a majority—over 60 percent of the extremely alienated citizens —expressed approval. In the welter of countless demonstrations, perhaps these changes in national opinion are not so surprising. It is striking, though, that protest politics have

115

FIGURE 6-1.
Percentage Approval of Legal Protest Meetings and Mass
Marches among the Most Allegiant and the Most Alienated
Americans, 1968-1972

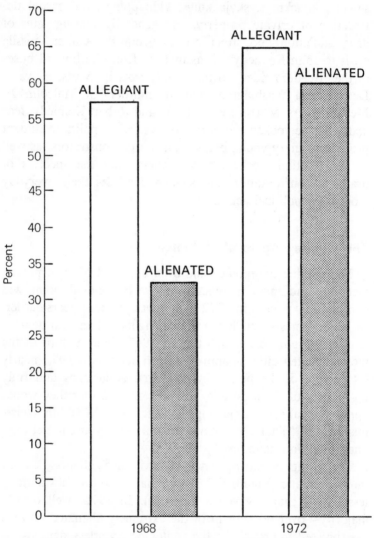

Percentage Who Approve Legal Protest Meetings and Marches

FIGURE 6-2.
Percentage Approval of Civil Disobedience among the
Most Allegiant and the Most Alienated Americans,
1968-1972

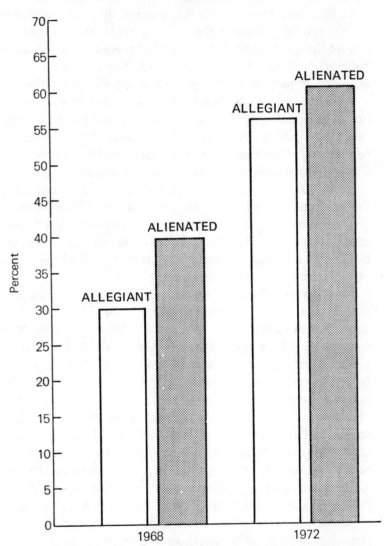

Percentage Who Approve Civil Disobedience—
Refusal to Obey an Unjust Law; Ready to Go to Jail for Beliefs

so rapidly become a fixture in American political life. In 1964 such tactics were new and thus did not arouse much debate.[3]

Perhaps the most remarkable change in public attitudes toward protest politics is the growing approval of "trying to disrupt the government" as a means of protesting government policies. As Figure 6-3 shows, in 1972 over 44 percent of the alienated Americans said they could support such violence as a political means, and nearly the same percent of governmentally supportive Americans said they could as well. At the time these opinions were gathered, a number of protests aimed to disrupt government operations had already occurred: the Berrigans' destruction of draft records, student sit-ins and riots against ROTC and military recruiters on college campuses, the confrontation at the Pentagon, and the 200,000-person civilian invasion aimed at disruption of governmental Washington, among others.[4] By 1972 many people had evidently begun to view such methods as potentially useful for their own circumstances and issues.

Mass protest, civil disobedience, and illegal disruption are now a part of the accepted political scene. When H. Rap Brown stated in the early 1960s that "violence is as American as apple pie," he was considered a radical, reckless, and dangerous figure. Ten years later, a majority of Americans appeared to agree with his statement. The outbreak of fist fights and at least two killings over almost empty gas pumps during the fuel crisis of 1973 surprised almost no one. And while strikes, and accompanying civil disobedience, by major industrial unions are, of course, not new, strikes and marches by sanitation workers, nurses, teachers, office workers, factory workers, bus drivers, waiters, peace groups, blacks, Indians, police, doctors, ambulance drivers, welfare mothers, elevator repairmen, firemen, postal workers now occur with increased frequency. The average American simply shrugs his shoulders and considers this part of the normal scene. As one New Yorker we talked to put it, "My favorite game in the City is

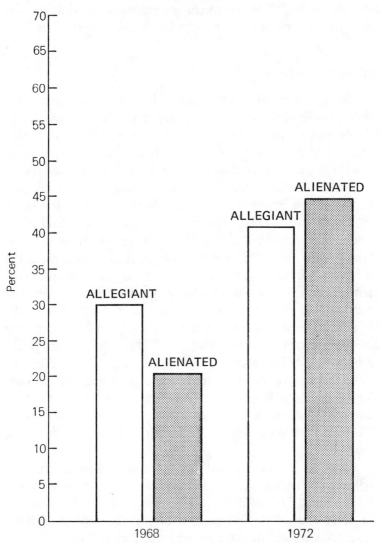

FIGURE 6-3.
Percentage Approval of Disruptive Protest among the
Most Allegiant and the Most Alienated Americans,
1968-1972

Percentage Who Approve Trying to Disrupt Normal
Government Operations to Protest Government Policies

waking up in the morning and trying to guess which vital public service will be out on strike today before turning on the morning news." The accompanying outbreaks of violence that tend to go along with these activities are shrugged off as well.

Alienated Opinion

The alienated Americans are only somewhat more likely than anyone else to approve the newer political forms of civil disobedience and protest tactics. But their opinions of contemporary social issues are markedly different from those in the mainstream of political thinking. By 1972, for most Americans, the cold war had faded into history, and the national focus was on international détente instead. Not so for many of the alienated. Asked whether the government should allow trade with Communist countries, nearly half of this group said, "No," while only 25 percent of the politically integrated felt this way.[5] Similarly, disillusioned and alienated people were more likely to disagree with the proposition that the government should give aid to countries that are "different from the U.S."[6] John Shearworth's comments are probably illustrative of many in this group: "Different? Does that mean giving money to the Communists? Not with my tax dollars! That just gives them more money to make more guns and ammunition. Then they'll be killing more American boys. . . . Anyway, I've seen that foreign aid when I was over there in the service. There isn't hardly any of it doesn't end up in the black market."

Asked in 1972 if "we did the right thing in getting into the fighting in Vietnam or should we have stayed out?" most Americans said: "Yes, we did the right thing," or "It depends," or "I don't know." But 64 percent of the alienated Americans said, "No, we should have stayed out." Judith Weissman said, "Of course we should have stayed out; it was an atrocity." On the other side, Aaron Rouse explained his answer, "If

120

we'd of dropped a couple of H-bombs up there in North Vietnam, we'd 've been out of there in two months. But the way we went at it, pussyfootin' around, we'd 've been better off stayin' the hell out of there." [7]

As the last two comments point out, while the alienated citizens may feel differently about public issues than others do, they don't necessarily agree with each other beyond their general cynicism and personal sense of inefficacy regarding contemporary government. In fact, they are likely to express strong differences of opinion about the way to proceed in dealing with any issue. Vietnam policy is a good example. In 1968 the presidential election survey asked whether respondents favored "immediate withdrawal," "complete military victory," or a policy "somewhere between the two extreme positions." Those who were extremely alienated in 1968 were twice as likely as others to urge immediate withdrawal, yet there were also many extreme hawks in this group. In other words, alienated opinion about Vietnam was much less likely to be moderate or middle-ground opinion.

This pattern of extreme feelings was repeated when questions were asked about core domestic issues. In 1968 people were asked what they thought was the best way "to deal with the problem of urban unrest and rioting." Offered a seven-point scale of choice ranging from "solve problems of poverty and unemployment" to "use all available force," the extreme positions proved more popular to the alienated than to others. The bellicose, "use all possible force" demand was almost three times as popular in this group. When the same question was repeated in 1972, the polarized responses of the alienated were even more pronounced. Well over half chose one of the two extreme solutions to the urban unrest problem. [8] One extreme position is illustrated by Ralph White, who said, "If you let them go on like that, they'll be looting right here, and nothing will stop them," while Sandra Minter took the other extreme: "Until we break this cycle of discrimination and

121

poverty we can never have peace in the cities." This was not a group with middle-of-the-road answers. Asked about busing children out of their neighborhood schools as a means of achieving racial integration, again, the alienated Americans were less likely to favor a middle-ground solution. Few citizens of any persuasion were likely to urge "busing to achieve integration," but the alienated citizen was more likely than others to take this position. At the same time, others of this estranged frame of mind were far more likely to say, "Keep children in neighborhood schools," than to take a more moderate stance.

Candidates of the Disillusioned

It should come as no surprise that the alienated Americans are independent in their politics; they're likely not to claim membership in either of the two major political parties. Repeatedly, we heard the refrain, "I think it's the man that really counts, not the party." The national election surveys support our finding. They consistently report that increasing numbers of disillusioned and politically estranged voters declined to state a party preference. In 1972 some 43 percent of the most alienated citizens said that they were "independents." This figure includes 15 percent of the alienated voters who refer to themselves either as "independent Democrats" or "independent Republicans." About 29 percent of the most allegiant citizens refer to themselves as "independent" on this basis.

Party independence does not mean blandness of political choice. On the contrary, the alienated voter was least likely to choose the traditionally safe, middle-of-the-road candidate. In 1964, although Senator Barry Goldwater suffered a devastating defeat in the presidential election (as Figure 6-4 shows), he earned more than his proportionate share of the alienated vote. Like Ralph White and John Shearworth, many of these voters were attracted to his no-nonsense style, his rugged individualism, and his defiant stand against communism. For

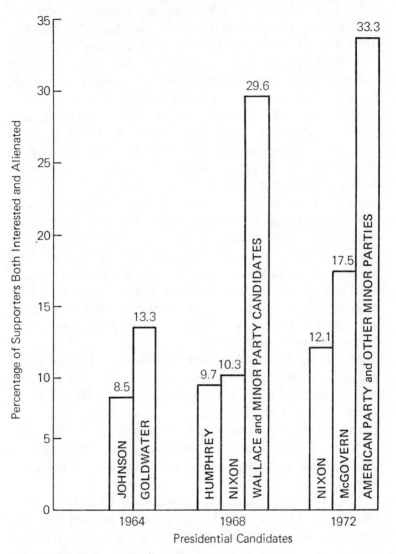

FIGURE 6-4.
Politically Interested but Extremely Alienated Voters as a Percentage
of Supporters for Presidential Candidates, 1964-1972

many, Goldwater's candidacy seemed to signal a genuine return of "moral fiber" to an ethically flabby political system.

Four years later, 70 percent of the alienated voters said that their first choice for the Democratic presidential nomination was either Robert Kennedy or Eugene McCarthy. Governor George Wallace was not on the list of possible choices since he was already the announced candidate of the American Independent Party. This was the year that both McCarthy and Kennedy made frontal attacks on President Lyndon B. Johnson, who was also the leader of their own political party. In New York City, we talked to Dave Stallings, who has always held political views well to the left of center. But in 1968 Kennedy was close enough to Dave's ideal. "Bobby had grown a tremendous amount since the days when he was the young Attorney General in the shadow of his big brother," Dave said. "I think he had really developed a vision of a different America, one that showed its true dependence on the working class and without the racism that is now so pervasive. I honestly believe he had that vision, more than his brother John ever did." In San Diego, Alan Arthur said he thought that "Gene McCarthy was like a breath of fresh air, the first one in a long while." Polled after President Johnson's decision not to run for reelection in 1968, only 20 percent of the alienated vote favored the heir apparent, Vice-President Hubert Humphrey. Yet it was Humphrey who eventually became the Party's nominee. As one disgusted junior high school teacher in Nassau County expressed his feelings: "Humphrey prostituted himself on the war issue in just about every conceivable way."

After a violent Democratic Convention in Chicago in 1968, many of the Kennedy and McCarthy supporters felt they had nowhere to turn. They stayed home on election day, and voter turnout percentages dipped. Others turned away from the Democratic Party entirely and voted for Governor George Wallace. As Figure 6-4 shows, nearly 30 percent of the support for Wallace and other minority party candidates came from the ranks of the politically disenchanted. Curiously, many of those who had backed Robert Kennedy before his assassination switched their support to Wallace and became the mainstays of Wallace's northern strength. Theodore White reports that, despite a massive and successful effort to put Wallace's American Independent Party on the ballot in all fifty states, no poll had shown him with more than 10 percent of the national vote during 1967 and early 1968. "Then, within days of the assassination of Robert F. Kennedy, the polling response to Wallace began to rise; and with the violence of the Chicago convention another jump in response was apparent. From 9 percent (April–May), Wallace moved to 16 percent (June), to 21 percent (mid-September), and by linear extrapolation would, if the trend continued unbroken, reach close to 30 percent by voting day!" [9] This did not happen, of course, and in fact Wallace's percentage of popular support dropped substantially before the November election.[10]

The left-right split for the presidency was even more pronounced in 1972. Though Governor Wallace was shot and critically wounded during his Democratic primary campaign in Maryland, he remained the popular hero in the minds of many voters. In this year, Wallace challenged traditional politics from within the Democratic Party. Nevertheless, the American Party he had founded remained on the ballot, headed by former California Congressman John G. Schmitz. Of those who voted for Schmitz or wrote in for the critically wounded Wallace, one-third expressed feelings of both extreme political alienation and a high degree of political interest. Others, whom we have called "reformers," were attracted to the more leftist candidacy of Senator George McGovern. Over 17 percent of McGovern's support came from the alienated but nonapathetic group. This was proportionally more than the number of "reformers" in the population at large.

125

Alienated Action

From this review of the political opinions and presidential candidates of alienated voters, it should be apparent that there are generally two types of people: those who have dropped out of national politics, because either they lost interest or they have decided to abstain temporarily, and those who maintain an active interest in national political life and continue to participate.

People who are still interested in politics, even though they strongly distrust national officeholders, feel powerless to change national government, believe that the two major political parties are meaningless, but still participate almost as actively in national politics as anyone else. They are only somewhat less likely to attend political meetings, wear campaign buttons, display bumper stickers, work for political candidates, or donate funds for political campaigns than anyone else. When the alienated Americans do participate, they are most likely to give their active support for the non-traditional issues and candidates.

What is much less clear is whether these citizens will become involved in the nontraditional forms of political action, the sit-ins, strikes, boycotts, mass marches, and the other forms of civil disobedience, violent demonstrations, and riots. The numbers of people actually participating in these political actions are so small that they turn up in sample surveys only rarely. We do know, however, that the most alienated Americans have recently been more prone than others to approve of civil disobedience and political violence, and that the groups most likely to express extreme alienation in the past have been the same ones that have used these tactics.

The Civil Rights Movement. In the early 1960s, black and white Americans began to organize as a political movement to guarantee civil rights, and they widely demonstrated

126

the effectiveness of disobedience in the face of unjust laws. Following the successes of legal tactics culminating with the U.S. Supreme Court's dramatic declaration against segregated education, extra-legal tactics emerged as the means to challenge other forms of racial discrimination. These protests were immediately broadcast to a large audience, and increasing thousands of people were drawn into a new kind of politics.[11]

The arrest in 1955 of Rosa Parks, who refused to give her seat to a white person on a Montgomery, Alabama bus, touched off not only a bitter, year-long black boycott of city buses but a series of civil rights incidents throughout the South as well. The legitimacy of government, law, and authority could scarcely have been brought more directly into question than in 1957: Arkansas Governor Orval Faubus attempted to block court-ordered integration of Little Rock Central High School. The intense local violence that erupted was quelled only after President Eisenhower federalized the Arkansas National Guard and sent in a thousand soldiers of the 101st Airborne Division of the United States Army to enforce the Court's edict through a virtual occupation of the entire school area.[12]

In 1960 black college students from the State Agricultural and Technical College at Greensboro, North Carolina, launched the first "sit-in." Their method of protest, at a dime-store lunchcounter, spread rapidly throughout the South and the border states. A year later, the "freedom rides," aimed at integrating interstate bus facilities in the South, ended in flaming violence at Anniston, Alabama. Greyhound placed other buses in service, but the "rides" ended in Jackson, Mississippi with a mass arrest of the riders. In that same state a year later, James Meredith was prevented from entering the University of Mississippi by a full-scare riot and a show of state force against another federal court order.[13]

In 1963, at Birmingham, Alabama, Martin Luther King's

127

Southern Christian Leadership Conference staged repeated protests against racial discrimination, and repeatedly their mass marches were met with police dogs, fire hoses, and arrest. In Mississippi, state NAACP leader Medgar Evers was shot in the back by a sniper one night as he returned home. During the same year, Governor George Wallace briefly attempted to block the integration of Alabama's schools, but in the face of an overwhelming display of federal force, he backed down. In late summer, more than 200,000 demonstrators converged in an interracial "March on Washington for Jobs and Freedom."

These protests and countless other incidents and counteractions culminated in the passage of a mild but nonetheless historic civil rights bill of 1957 and eventually the far stronger and more important Civil Rights Act of 1964. These events also figured in the victory of Senator Goldwater as the Republican presidential nominee and his successful showing in the general elections in five southern states. Advances by the civil rights movement also laid the groundwork for a surprisingly powerful counterthrust by Alabama Governor Wallace in 1968.

The Antiwar Movement. The enormous protest movement against the Vietnam war in many ways took off from and then eclipsed the civil rights movement. It too began with limited incidents; it gradually enlarged and became broader in scope. It culminated in the formation of groups that held "teach-ins," coordinated mass marches in major cities, led prayer vigils, organized sit-ins, and took part in many scenes of violent confrontation.[14]

U.S. forces had been marginally involved in the Vietnam war for at least a decade when, in 1965, American force levels, armaments, and casualties in Southeast Asia mushroomed.[15] These events touched off a national debate that was to last for most of another decade. As the tempo of the war increased with full-scale American involvement in ground fighting and sustained aerial bombardment of both South and North Vietnam, the tempo of antiwar protest at home also increased. Opposition to the war grew through "teach-ins" on college campuses and in public forums across the country. Sporadic demonstrations became increasingly frequent, and in the fall of 1965, for three days between October 15–17, an estimated 70,000 people participated in mass marches and protest rallies in sixty cities. Little more than a month later, an estimated 20,000 demonstrators staged a nonviolent "March on Washington for Peace in Vietnam."

Despite mounting dissatisfaction at home, the Johnson administration vastly increased the scope of its commitment to the war in 1966. The number of U.S. forces was nearly doubled—to a total of 385,300. By the end of 1967, there were 458,600 American troops in Vietnam, not including an additional 83,000 in Thailand and the offshore fleet.[16] Toward the end of October 1967, some 55,000 people gathered for a weekend of protest at the steps of the Pentagon, just across the Potomac River from the Capitol. For the most part, the demonstration was peaceful, but occasional violence did erupt during the two-day confrontation.[17]

As both the military stalemate and the intensity of domestic dissent continued, pressures on the Johnson administration clearly began to reach unbearable levels as election year 1968 approached. The President was greeted by hostile, jeering audiences wherever he appeared. Chants of "Hey, Hey, LBJ! How many kids did you kill today?" colored the background for many of the President's remaining public appearances and the sound tracks of the nightly television news.

On November 30, 1967, Democratic Senator Eugene McCarthy announced that he would oppose the President and leader of his own political party in the forthcoming presidential primaries. Less than three and a half months later, after a youthful, antiwar and pro-McCarthy blitz of New

Hampshire, the Senator showed surprising strength in the presidential primary of that state. This challenge to the war and to the existing leadership drew others into the primary contests, most notably Senator Robert Kennedy of New York. Governor George Wallace also joined the fray, taking an even more militant stand against the Vietcong and North Vietnamese Communists than the incumbent administration had. Despite these events, it was still a surprise when President Johnson declared on March 31, 1968, that he had no intention of running for reelection. During the same speech, the President announced an unconditional bombing halt, signaling a deescalation of the war. With this announcement, at least one of the aims of the antiwar movement had been accomplished.

Momentum Yields to Violence. Neither the civil rights movement nor the antiwar movement ended quietly once major objectives had been achieved. The momentum generated by each was brought to heel only after the tumult of mass violence in the streets had run its course. No doubt the new consciousness developed and the expectations raised by the generally peaceful civil rights demonstrations played a considerable role in the rioting, looting, and devastation of black ghetto areas, even after the Civil Rights Act had been signed into law. The rioting, destruction, and police violence that occurred at the Democratic Convention in Chicago in 1968 and on major college campuses around the country in 1968 and 1969 followed President Johnson's decision to step down and to end a Vietnam policy predicated on military victory.

Both of these movements developed and expanded over a considerable period of time and according to relatively similar stages. First, frustration began to be felt by large numbers of people as the problem and its effects became widely identified. Second, new groups formed to spread the message of

130

dissent and carry the call to political action still farther, and existing groups picked up the issue as their own. For example, once the antiwar movement was well launched and rapidly drawing strength from the centers of civil rights support, Martin Luther King proposed that the two movements merge in order to retain a hold on groups and social sectors that had begun to change their focus. Third, conflicts and confrontations developed as the goals of each movement were clarified, and opposition forces began to respond. Finally, when expectations raised by the movement could not be fulfilled, even by the attainment of primary goals, outright violence erupted.[18] In some instances, legally constituted authorities precipitated the violence of otherwise passive protesters and demonstrators; in others, the heavy handedness of the police was used to put down civil violence; and in still others, the police exercised restraint, standing by in a line of containment until the violence had run its course.[19]

To a considerable extent, Americans have lived through these events as first-hand observers of this "news theater" via the medium of television.[20] Often enough, the TV version offered the viewer spliced film footage shot from different angles or different locations, giving the impression of greater and more intense violence than actually occurred. Ignoring such distortions, however, the majority of Americans have become so thoroughly inundated by the domestic violence portrayed nightly on the news, and the gore of surrounding programming, that it is not surprising that a near majority now approves of disruptive protest as a means of political expression.

It should be reiterated that it is uncertain whether the men and women in the civil rights and antiwar movements or those in the "backlash" to each were the alienated Americans we have written about in this book. Most people, of course, did not become involved in any of these activities. But those who did and who actively commented on their participation expressed much the same estrangement, distrust, and sense of disdain for the traditional political parties and choices as did those people in our samples

Renunciation

The most drastic index of alienated political action is made up of those Americans who have renounced their citizenship. Formal renunciations have increased during the last quarter century, from 149 in 1950 to 320 in 1973, reaching a peak in 1968, at the height of United States involvement in the Vietnam war, when 679 Americans renounced their citizenship.[21]

These still minuscule figures of formal renunciation only begin to reflect the informal defection of Americans to other countries. Americans traveling in Canada, Mexico, Europe, and many other places almost invariably meet fellow country-men who make declarations something like that of a bar owner we met on a Bahama "out island" who said, "I've been living here for years now. . . . I have no need to go back to the States. There's nothing I want there." Some have permanent work abroad; others are sustained in their foreign retirements by social security checks; and still others are doing whatever they can simply to "stay away" for as long as possible.

The Vietnam war was by far the strongest impetus to American emigration in recent times. In 1969 the Army desertion rate rose to more than 29 per 1,000 men. "When I split," one deserter in Sweden said, "there was nothing else to do. . . . I had a choice—jail, Vietnam, or Sweden." [22] Government sources estimated that some 25,000 deserters and draft evaders remained outside the United States in 1974. Antiwar sources scoff at these figures, saying that as many as 50,000 war resisters reside in Canada alone.[23]

Many war resisters have now applied for foreign citizenship. A draft evader from Riverside, California, now in Toronto, Canada, commented, "Freedom to travel in the States is more important to most of us than American citizenship." [24] Another who deserted the Army rather than go to Vietnam said, "Canada is a fantastic place to live. If they want to give me a dishonorable discharge for refusing to kill, I'd be happy. I'd like to put it on my wall along with my [Canadian] law degree." [25] Others, like Bill Terry, who we talked to at length, left for Canada not because they were evading the draft but because they were "fed up" with conditions and with the general "climate" in America. In fact, a breakdown by age and sex of those who qualified as "landed," or permanent, immigrants to Canada at the height of war resistance showed that draft age men alone did not account for the increasing numbers.

Bill Terry related his determination to live in a morally healthier society: "There's lots of good things happening in Canada—a lot better feeling, better vibrations." Unlike many exiles who were fleeing the draft, Bill served his time in Vietnam. He came back "wiped out" by the experience. He describes the drug scene in the military division in which he served as "one big trip out," with the officers, as well as the enlisted men, not only taking drugs but selling, transporting, and smuggling them back to the States and throughout the Far East. Even if one discounts these stories, the lack of official morality and the insanity of the war itself did lead Bill and others like him to reject "the system" that was at fault.

Bill is content to live and work as a welder in British Columbia. During his five years there, he has made numerous efforts to help other Americans get settled in their new environment. He knows that many draft evaders and deserters would accept amnesty and come back to the United States if they could be sure there would be no reprisals. But his own experience leads him to think, "A lot of those guys will take amnesty just so they can go back and see their relatives. I can't believe many of them will want to stay." He says, "You just get strung out back there. You can't live a natural life in the States."

A Question of Legitimacy

Social theorist Lewis Coser has written that "when a social structure is no longer considered legitimate, individuals with similar objective positions will come, through conflict, to constitute themselves into self-conscious groups with common interests." [26] Whether the legitimacy of the general social structure was called into question by the civil rights movement is debatable, but certain aspects of it definitely were. It also seems certain that the legitimacy of prevailing southern (and to some extent national) policy was believed to be illegitimate by large segments of the population. In some limited areas of the South, of course, the once prevailing white power structure has since been replaced by a black power structure.

In the antiwar protests that followed, not only was the policy of war objected to, but the legitimacy of the government's conduct was challenged. No less a figure than Supreme Court Justice Potter Stewart raised the question: "Is the present United States military activity in Vietnam a 'war' within the meaning of Article I, Section 8, Clause 11 of the Constitution? . . . If so, may the Executive constitutionally order the petitioners to participate in that military activity when no war has been declared by Congress?" [27] More radical figures openly raised the question of the legitimacy of the government to conduct "this lawless war." In 1970, when President Nixon ordered a large-scale air and ground attack into neutral Cambodia, his use of presidential authority was questioned by many people who had never before given much thought to the matter. Many thousands of students, including a large number of high school students, became personally

134

involved in the waves of protest that followed and that finally culminated in the demonstration and slaughter at Kent State University.[28]

Apart from the divisive issues and movements that have created turmoil during the last two decades, there is a less focussed but growing public feeling that we now have a government that is wasteful, out of touch, incapable, overly powerful, and out of control. When asked about the importance of elections during the 1972 presidential campaign, over 40 percent of the potential voters said that elections don't have "much" effect or "only some" effect. About 64 percent of the public felt that congressmen "quickly lose touch" with the people who elect them, and nearly 60 percent said that political parties are interested in votes, not opinions. A look at Figure 6-5 shows that these opinions are strongly associated with the general cynicism that is part of the alienated response to politics. Yet a surprisingly large number of the most allegiant citizens hold these opinions as well (see Figure 6-6).

Other questions in the 1972 survey revealed feelings that appear to go beyond cynicism. When asked whether they thought government people are capable, about 40 percent answered, 'No." Over a majority of the extremely alienated respondents felt this way. Many of the people we talked to cited instances from their own experience of bureaucratic incompetence, stupidity, corruption, or some combination of the three. Harry Sindler, for example, told us a number of anecdotes to illustrate these feelings. Harry owns a small corporation that manufactures plastic products in Hialeah, Florida. When he was asked about the competence of government officials, he recalled his attempt to respond to numerous government ads urging the employment of returning Vietnam veterans. At the time his business was flourishing and he had hoped to employ some veterans who needed work. The results were as follows:

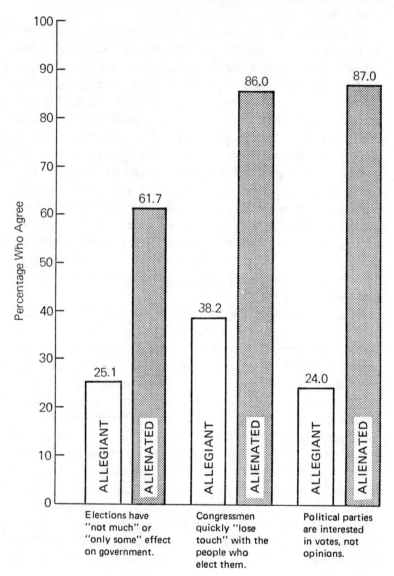

FIGURE 6-5.
Opinions about Elections, Congressmen, and Political Parties among the Most Allegiant and the Most Alienated Americans (in percentages), 1972

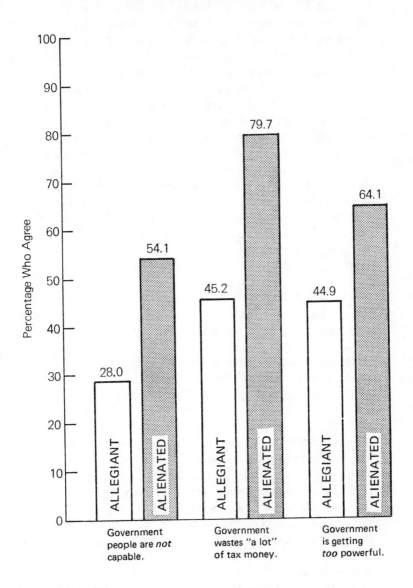

FIGURE 6-6.
Opinions about Government among the Most Allegiant
and the Most Alienated Americans (in percentages), 1972

Percentage Who Agree

28.0 — ALLEGIANT
54.1 — ALIENATED
Government people are *not* capable.

45.2 — ALLEGIANT
79.7 — ALIENATED
Government wastes "a lot" of tax money.

44.9 — ALLEGIANT
64.1 — ALIENATED
Government is getting *too* powerful.

Political Alienation

First of all, the agency you had to call was in Miami. Now
this plant is in Hialeah, the industrial section that's right
next door where most of the plants hiring workers are. I
mentioned that I had seen the advertising in the newspaper
and on the television in regards to giving the vets a job
and asked if they would send me three veterans.

They did not ask the pay; they did not ask what the
working conditions were; there were absolutely no questions
whatsoever. Well, they finally did ask what the address
of this plant was, and I was told over the phone that it was,
just too far away, that they couldn't send men that far for a job.

I thought it was ridiculous, but there again, someone's
getting paid to do the advertising, there are so many people
getting paid on the administration of these organizations
that they didn't want to get these veterans a job; they just
wanted to hold on to their own jobs. We're back to the same
old story; if it's political, it's gonna cost you ten times
more than private industry would charge you.

Asked about the government's possible waste of tax money,
Harry told us about the problems he and other independent
businessmen have been having with the mails:

With my personal experience with the mails, and that of
my business friends and other acquaintances, it's just about
impossible to try and figure out where the mail is going.
I honestly believe they're burning it. They lose so much
of it, that just has to be it. The letters are stamped; there's
a return address in the corner. You mail sometimes three
and four letters to the same party; they never receive
them, and you never get them back. Now, where are they?

We once had a mailman at another plant who came in one
day and asked, "What size shoe do you take?" I told
him, and he said, "Oh, these won't fit you." This mailman
had, in the boxes they came in, eighteen pairs of shoes
that had never been on his feet. He wanted to sell them to
me cheap. These shoes are government issue. Now that's
one mailman with eighteen pairs of shoes. Multiply that by

how many hundred thousand mailmen there are (God
only knows) and now you begin to know why letters cost
ten cents apiece and why they lose them.

He would stop in my plant, ask if he could come in where
the air conditioner was to cool off. I said, "Fine." He'd go
outside; he'd let the air out of his tires. Because this took
between two and a half and three hours before they'd send
a man to fix his flat tire, it meant he got so many hours
overtime, and he was making money on that, too. He also,
in a joking way, asked if I'd like to buy some earmuffs,
which the government issues him. Earmuffs are not the thing
I need for South Florida. Now this sounds like a joke,
but if you multiply how many thousand mailmen by eighteen
pairs of shoes they'll never wear, and earmuffs in South
Florida, you wonder where your money goes. Again, it's
political.

In 1972 almost 80 percent of the most alienated people felt,
like Harry, that the government wastes "a lot" of their tax
dollars. Nearly half of even the most allegiant Americans felt
the same way.

When people were asked whether the government is getting
too powerful, about 58 percent said that it was. Harry Sindler
described his feelings on the subject in terms of taking on a
government contract. He has done this before, but now, even
though the Navy Department has expressed an interest in a
large order, he wants no part of it:

My reason for not dealing with the government, regardless
of what department or anything, is simply that there is
entirely too much red tape. They give you a good markup;
they give you a good profit on it. But there are just too
many inspectors. Half the inspectors you have to buy. If you
don't, you're gonna run into trouble; they're gonna reject
this and reject that. It's just too political. In my estimation,
most politicians are crooked, and I just don't want to
deal with them.

139

Others told of dealing with welfare case workers, police, social security adjusters, and the Internal Revenue Service, but the feelings—always about "Them"—were the same. They're in control and out of control at the same time. The feeling that "the government," or simply "they," have "no right" to do much of what is done every day by government officialdom is widespread, but these feelings are still largely unfocused. There appears to be a latent sense that the government may no longer be *legitimate* in the eyes of the governed. Even so, as David Easton has pointed out, it is possible for political leaders to exercise authority even after those below them no longer consider this power to be legitimate. Easton explains it this way: "The members may accept the authorities, not because they believe them to be right and proper but because it is necessary or expedient for them to do so. Persons in positions of political leadership and administration may be able to get others to carry out their intention simply because on grounds of custom, expediency, self-interest, or fear it pays the others to do so." [29] The United States may not yet have reached this point but it appears to be well on its way. Unless there is a decided change in direction, the illegitimate state Easton describes may be an inevitable American reality.

chapter 7
The Edge of Allegiance

Islands of Hope

"There may be islands of hope across this broad land of ours, but a central fact is that as a nation, as a people, disaffection and disenchantment abound at every turn. For the first time in over a decade of opinion sampling, this survey shows that disaffection has now reached majority proportions." This was the crux of Louis Harris's testimony before Congress in December 1973. The well-known national pollster went on to explain:

> On a scale of powerlessness, cynicism, and alienation used by the Harris firm since 1966, an average of 55% of the American people expressed disenchantment, compared with no more than 29% who felt that way only seven years ago. This trend has been steadily and almost unabatingly upward from 29% in 1966 to 36% in 1968 to 42% in 1971 to 49% in 1972 to 55% in 1973, a veritable floodtide of disenchantment, seemingly gaining momentum with each passing year.[1]

Our more conservatively derived figures have shown that in 1972 nearly a quarter of our citizens were extremely alienated. If we add all the people who answered at least three of our scale questions indicating political disenchantment, the percentage of disillusioned and alienated Americans would be nearly 80 percent, and over 90 percent in some quarters. Feelings of disenchantment are especially prevalent among blacks and the elderly, as well as among white, lower income working people. These are indeed the "forgotten Americans" who have been politically neglected and economically bypassed. Caught short by marginally declining purchasing power in the trail of soaring inflation, this disenchantment hardly comes as a surprise. What is surprising is the widespread and rapidly growing sense of disillusion and extreme disenchantment among the very people who had been the government's most contented followers and strongest supporters in the past. Many of the well-to-do and well educated, often successful professionals or private businessmen, like Judith Weissman, Deryl and Sandra Minter, and the Alan Arthurs, have now joined the ranks of the extremely alienated. In past years, they might have felt that some of the opinions they now express were radical or even un-American. Time and recent governmental performance have changed all that.

There are still "islands of hope" in the country. Men and women like Byron Vining, Arnold and Emily Dryden, and Rachael Morrison continue to thrive in their organizational settings and surrounding social environments. They have largely accepted the values inherent there and adjusted their lives accordingly. In 1972 about 20 percent of our citizens expressed a firm belief in the veracity and meaning of American politics. But this number has steadily declined for more than a decade. Independent businessmen, such as Aaron Rouse and Harry Sindler, have become increasingly distressed with the business conditions they have to deal with and the general tone of the country. Today they tie these observations directly to political malpractice. Harry Sindler puts it this way: "I dislike politicians with a passion. I will till the day I

142

die, because I believe 99 out of every 100 of 'em are crooked.
I believe that they will vote not for the good of the country
but for anything to fatten their own pockets. I am not the most
honest person in the world, but compared to these guys, I'm a
babe in the woods."

Some people, like Sharon McRae, have become so disillusioned by the government's failure to respond to their
genuine needs that they have given up and withdrawn; many
more like Jenny Jackson, Sherman Woods, Ralph and Joyce
White, and the Arthurs, are still interested and continue to
follow public affairs and elections, but they no longer see any
point in voting. For the time being, they have abstained.
Still others, like Judith Weissman, John Shearworth, and the
Minters, continue to participate, voting for marginal candidates and parties and hoping for meaningful reform within
the traditional system. In view of these people and the growing numbers of Americans who share their views, Louis Harris's stern warning must be taken seriously. "The American
people are far from apathetic, uninterested in the public affairs of their country, or uninvolved," he said. "It is only at
their peril that public officials assume an apathetic public, or
one which will not respond." [2] It is not only this disaffection
that has spread rapidly among Americans; as a nation we have
tutored our young to be estranged from leadership and authority and to readily accept violent behavior.

The Children of Watergate

For the better part of a generation, America's children have
grown up with the scuffle of dissent and mass demonstrations
and the raucous fury of city and campus riots, all presented
almost blandly as evening entertainment. Public persons, once
infrequent visitors to our thoughts and dimly revered as potential statesmen, are now nightly intruders into our homes.
Predictably, they mouth the same banalities, squint outrage

at the same charges of corruption, and urge our sacrifice for yet another crisis or war. But there are charges and epithets they never hear, hurled at uncomprehending television screens by disenchanted constituents. The voices of the voiceless lay bare these would-be "statesmen" as "bums" and "crooks" and "unindicted felons," while children sit by, waiting for the next edition of "Kung Fu" or "Maddigan." Little they learn from the TV would effectively contradict parental cues. Increasingly, this is the manner of political socialization of the young.

Leading social theorists have consistently emphasized the positive aspects of social structure that are impressed upon children from birth through adolescence by parents and other reinforcing institutions outside the family.[3] Most would agree that socializing processes are vital to a system's strength and long-term survival;[4] yet many of these activities are carried out unconsciously, and sometimes by children themselves.

Until recently, the possibility of *negative* or *ambivalent* political socialization of the young was almost totally ignored. David Easton and Jack Dennis were among the first to recognize this possibility in the aftermath of the 1968 civil rights protests, ghetto riots, and student demonstrations.[5] On the basis of their sample of children's attitudes, they argue: "Even if later events should disillusion members about the structure of authority, the rate of decline in support might at least be restrained somewhat by the pull of latent childhood sentiments."[6] In other words, the fundamental assumption has been that the political socialization process will continue much as before, inculcating positive values toward political leaders and other authority figures. Indeed, the prime conception is one in which the child will become imbued with the prevailing tenets of social morality, obedient to laws, aware and respectful of government and its leaders, and precocious in role identification and emulation. Here the trickle of doubt begins. What would be the result if children fail to develop positive identification with government officialdom and other figures

144

of authority, or worse, if they develop negative images? And what of black children after generations of domination and neglect who now face a rising racial awareness?

Before 1974 the few studies completed in this area concluded that white and black children responded alike to the major identifiable authority figures—the President and policemen—in terms of glowing approval.[7] But after a decade of civil rights and Vietnam protests, culminating in the unfolding Watergate scandals, the positive or negative direction of socialization is unclear. No doubt pluses and minuses act on youngsters simultaneously, but, as Christopher Arterton has observed in a post-Watergate study of children's attitudes, there has been a significant change in the overall pattern: "the president does not merely receive less positive ratings than in 1962, but he receives *negative* ratings." [8] This negative response reaches well beyond the presidency. "Comparing 1973 and 1962," Arterton finds, "politicians are seen as more selfish, less intelligent, more dishonest, and less likely to keep their promises." [9]

These results led Arterton to conclude: "The responses of children in 1973 indicate an entirely different experience in political socialization from the reports of earlier research." [10] In large measure, these changed perceptions probably reflect the disenchantment and political distrust expressed by parents. It is now something of a political truism that children follow the examples of their parents in their own political choices in adult life.[11] Evidently, the process of political opinion change and pattern emulation has been speeded up by recent events.

If Easton and Dennis and others are correct in their assertion that the President is a central figure both to the child's focus for political authority and to the broad-based development of system support, then we might well be about to embark on an entirely new epoch in which the path of change will be strewn more frequently with "open and violent conflict," and "even the style of political participation will shift

145

radically from debate, the hustings, and the ballot box to the street, the bullet, and the torch." [12] Based on evidence at the height of the Watergate drama, Arterton argues that "for a generation we should see a substantial impairment of the legitimacy upon which the stability of our political system is based." [13] It may well be that the enduring distinction of the Nixon administration will not be the "opening to the East" or "a generation of peace" or even the sordid episodes of corruption and misuse of power, but instead a vital breakdown in the political system's socialization of its youngest members.

Political Polarization

As traumatizing as the misbehavior of the Nixon administration has been, alienating forces already at work in America may allow a shorter leadtime for dramatic change than that required for the political maturation of Watergate's children. Spreading disaffection for the contemporary practices of American politics is already widely shared by adults who fundamentally disagree on the appropriate responses to the most pressing national problems. On the critical issues of race and poverty and on the international difficulties of dealing with Communist and other powers in the nuclear age, opinions of the alienated are far more polarized and extreme than those of other citizens.

Even at a relatively low level of intensity, political polarization is a serious obstacle to the development of consensus for effective national policy. At its extreme, polarization threatens the *modus operandi* of compromise, and eventually the very stability of society. Political polarization has held devastating consequences for societies unable to contain its threat, such as Germany during the later years of the Weimar Republic and pre-Civil War America.

In America, the compromise system is endemic to politics at every level. The framing of the Constitution is itself aptly

146

described in most elementary texts as a "bundle of compromises." And in the councils of decision making, formal votes are typically anticlimatic to the more meaningful and subtle maneuvers of consensus building. The compromise system is imperfect; some participants are excluded, and others labor under severe political disabilities of poverty, ignorance, and disorganization.[14] Yet the system has shown its ability to expand its boundaries over the years, and it is probably more responsive to dissident outcries than most.

Despite the importance of the compromise system to American government as we have known it and to the stability of any democratic society, political compromise has come under incessant attack for more than a decade. Often the most substantial thrusts are launched by the system's professed supporters. At times, this attack has been forthright and direct. Senator Barry Goldwater, for instance, made his politics of no compromise a presidential platform in 1964. In a ringing declaration on acceptance of the Republican nomination, Goldwater concluded: *"Extremism in the defense of liberty is no vice! . . . Moderation in the pursuit of justice is no virtue!"* [15]

More commonly, the attack on compromise has been less obvious, often invisible, or even unintended. A prime example is the sustained degrading of the political party system by the press and television and at the street-corner level by many people. The parties are repeatedly pictured as corrupt, unnecessary, and probably unhealthy for the body politic. Yet historically they have allowed rapid upward mobility for members of America's newly arrived minorities as well as ethnic representation in government. Through the ticket-balancing mechanism, both parties have ameliorated competitive ethnic group demands for political access and power. They have also balanced a wide array of opinions and ideological fragments, thus achieving substantial adjustment of conflict well before electoral events pit one party against another.[16] This aspect of

147

the "tweedle-dum" and "tweedle-dee" variety of party system was widely if only briefly appreciated during the presidential contest of 1964, when for an historic moment the Republican party narrowed its ideological focus. Compromises engineered by the national parties are not the end-all of political life, but national institutional replacements to satisfy the conflicting demands of groups and factions have yet to make an appearance.

Despite the contrast and often violent clash of opposing points of view on critical issues in America, consensus-building figures have rarely risen to places of public prominence and esteem. Political party leaders in America appear to be incapable of presenting themselves as anything more than balloon releasers, cigar smoking buffoons, and worse. Popular figures, such as Ché Guevara, Moshe Dayan, and Curtis LeMay, appear as glorifications of simplistic solutions. Performers in highly visible negotiating roles, such as Theodore Kheel and Henry Kissinger, are the exceptions to the rule.[17] Our celluloid and kinescope heroes are quite often men and women who would evidently drop a "couple of H-bombs" on North Vietnam, or anywhere else, if only they could play for internationally large stakes. Robert Heilbroner suggests that such missions may not be confined to the realm of entertainment. With the continued spread of nuclear weapons, he predicts they may, in the foreseeable future, "be used as an instrument of blackmail to force the developed world to undertake a massive transfer of wealth to the poverty-stricken world."[18]

In our present-day reality, a startlingly large number of Nixon's minions proved adept at imitating their TV models. The real-life antics of E. Howard Hunt, G. Gordon Liddy, James McCord, Donald Segretti, and the remainder of Nixon's political burglars and cloak-and-dagger practitioners were shocking to many. Yet in a world filled with nightly visions of violence and corruption, many of the reactions we heard were nonplussed: "It's nothing different than any of the rest of them have done" or "What did you expect; it's politics." In a time of troubles and genuine crisis, a population steeped in cynicism, inured to violence, and supportive of extreme political solutions is hardly a stable base for democratic survival.

The Economic Basis

Just over forty years ago, A. A. Berle and Gardner C. Means sent shock waves throughout the world when they documented the increasing accumulation of wealth and productive power in the hands of a decreasing number of American corporations.[19] In 1967 John Kenneth Galbraith hardly shocked anyone when he began his latest book with a comment on that continuing trend:

> Seventy years ago the corporation was still confined to
> those industries—railroading, steamboating, steel-making,
> petroleum recovery and refining, some mining—where,
> it seemed, production had to be on a large scale. Now it
> also sells groceries, mills grain, publishes newspapers and
> provides public entertainment, all activities that were
> once the province of the individual proprietor or the
> insignificant firm. The largest firms deploy billions of
> dollars' worth of equipment and hundreds of thousands of men
> in scores of locations to produce hundreds of products.
> The five hundred largest corporations produce close to
> half of all the goods and services that are available annually
> in the United States.[20]

In 1973, one-tenth of 1 percent of America's 1.5 million corporations controlled over 55 percent of all corporate assets. Each field of production is dominated by at most a handful of conglomerates and perhaps by just one or two, in almost classic oligopolistic fashion. Price parities are finely tuned, usually without the awkward and illegal mechanisms of price

149

fixing per se, but with a careful eye both to industry price leaders and to government regulation.[21]

The government plays a sizable role in the economy, which further debases the free market. As John Kenneth Galbraith has written: "The industrial system, in fact, is inextricably associated with the state. And the state, in important matters, is an instrument of the industrial system." [22] Galbraith allows that this is not the "accepted doctrine." But since the New Deal, the government has had to develop agencies—SEC, TVA, FHA, OPA, WPA, BMB, COLC, FEO, to name but a few—to regulate one sector or another of the economy. As Robert Heilbroner sees it, starting with the New Deal, government "began to be envisioned not only as a regulator of markets, but as a *permanent* stabilizing and growth-promoting agency for the market economy as a whole." [23] Government "bailouts" of the Penn Central Railroad and Grumman and Lockheed aircraft companies in the fact of their recent economic difficulties are telling examples.

Since the 1930s labor has joined this configuration. But again, it is not simply labor but big labor organizations—the AFL-CIO, the Teamsters, UMW, UAW, the AFT, and the like—that have entered the councils of planning and decision. When President Ford held his widely heralded "summit conference on inflation," billed to embrace "all sectors of the economy," the only labor representatives were from the major labor unions which represent only a quarter of the American labor force.[24] Richard Goodwin argues that union managers, as well as corporate managers, "are linked by the immanent interest of the corporation itself—to function, grow, and earn. *The nature of their power and property requires each of them—including unions—to act consistently with the purpose, the inbuilt tropisms, of the economic bureaucracy.* This is true regardless of what particular individuals think they are doing or what they want to do." [25]

150

Yet the system of decision and influence is by no means monolithic. As in production, policy-making is specialized. Giant corporations are organized by divisions and subsidiaries as to the products they produce; so are the large unions that man their shops; so are the government agencies that regulate their production, sales, and use. What is more, all are inclined to guard jealously their jurisdictional prerogatives. Goodwin writes about his own experience near the pinnacle of governmental power: "Within government the fiercest battles are waged, not over principles and ideas, but for jurisdiction, for control of old and new programs." [26] Similar struggles take place within the large private conglomerates and the unions.

Congressional committees and subcommittees are also specialized to match their executive agency counterparts. The result, in terms of economic organization, is a set of relatively autonomous triumvirates—congressional committees, executive agencies, and economic clientele groups—or "subsystems" that are loosely coordinated by the Office of Management and Budget and the White House Staff.[27] On a day-to-day basis, these policy systems largely dominate their own areas of concern, and the critical interchanges occur between the public and private bureaucrats at the appropriate levels of their respective organizations. Business associations and big labor have a considerable voice here as the essential constituencies of the specialized units of Congress and the executive agencies. These are the confederations of private and public power that plan the American economy.

The traditional small firms and independent entrepreneurs are all but excluded from this process. Byron Vining barely comprehends the existence of such a system, since his insurance and second-home development interests have been able to prosper on the fringe of the system. Harry Sindler sees the system clearly for what it is, realizes his small company isn't bureaucratically equipped to participate, and wants no part of

151

it anyway. Others, feeling the pinch of 1974's tight money market and inflation, complain bitterly of bureaucrats and the "great government ripoff."

The economic and organizational system has been wholly predicated on fiscal growth and institutional expansion. In the constructs of classical economics, if there is "the absence of an expansionary frontier, the investment drive slows down and a recessionary spiral of incomes and employment begins. . . . Expansion serves an indispensable purpose in maintaining a socially acceptable level of employment and demand in laissez-faire capitalism." [28] In Galbraith's view of the contemporary economic structure, the "primary purpose" of the "technostructure" is "the growth of the firm. Such growth then becomes a major purpose of the planning system and, in consequence, of the society in which the large firm is dominant." [29] This generalization of the growth ethic applies equally to the governmental agency, the college department, and the expansion of money and debt. To the near panic of higher education bureaucrats, many colleges have fallen on hard times since 1968, and desperately desired expansions did not materialize. Yet the expansion of most government agencies appears to remain axiomatic, and money and debt expansions during the 1960s and early 1970s have achieved phenomenal new highs.

A Time of Trials

Most Americans need little reminding that the boundary between prosperous optimism and hopeless despair for the economic future may be crossed in a matter of months. Those who lived through the Depression of the 1930s well remember the crashing plummet of American confidence between 1929 and 1931. Recently stockholders have felt some of the same sense of panic as they watched paper values of their "best stocks" drop to 50 and 40 percent of their former values during the market devaluation of 1973–1974. For many of these investors, more than paper values were involved. Some had put in cash at the peak, and others found themselves selling and borrowing in order to meet margin calls. Yet most of them had much more to lose than their counterparts of the 1920s. Regardless of the current buffer of wealth, grave doubts have begun to intrude upon the security and hope of the recent past. Robert Heilbroner believes that there exists a shared "awareness of an oppressive anticipation of the future," which seems to be the result of "a barrage of confidence-shaking events that have filled us with a sense of unease and foreboding during the past decade or so." [30]

The trials which appear to loom ahead for America and the rest of the Western world are of several frightening orders. Potentially, the most destructive is global war. That threat persists despite the easing of cold war bluster and brinksmanship. The emerging prospect of détente may have superficially soothed our fears, but expenditures for war preparation continue to assume gargantuan proportions in national budgets throughout the world. The proliferation of nuclear weaponry has so distressed the atomic scientists that in 1974 their association moved forward the hands of the doomsday clock to nine minutes of midnight.[31] Perhaps there is some comfort in the fact that the threat of nuclear attack is one problem to which society has devoted its utmost attention. Unfortunately, the unceasing propagation of multileveled "deterrent" forces has been the only agreed means of solution.

The appearance of Rachel Carson's *Silent Spring* in 1962 alerted Americans to the dangers of widespread and indiscriminate use of agricultural chemicals.[32] Earth Day 1970, and its successors over several years, carried these warnings much more broadly: the danger of chlorinated hydrocarbons moving up the food chain; heavy metals pollution of the national water supply; the death of natural lakes and streams because of man-stimulated eutrophication; the threat of SSTs to man's psyche and property on land and the protective ozone layer above; the rapid disappearance of vital estuarine areas; the lethal challenge of increasing and virtually uncontainable atomic wastes; the continued depletion of timber reserves; untold varieties of carcinogenic substances carefully prepared as food and not so carefully dumped into the atmosphere; the threat of population explosion and world famine.[33] The list seemed horrifyingly endless. Then in 1972 the internationally prestigious Club of Rome released its report *The Limits to Growth*. Based on computer projections, the report concluded that if continued, the world's penchant for exponential growth will lead inexorably to world disaster.[34] In the United States, the report was met with skepticism and even derision, but the possibility of a finite resource base became more plausible during the winter fuel-related shortages of 1973–1974. Still, sophisticated street opinion understood that the "energy crisis" was engineered by the Arabs and the international oil companies in search of greater profits. Whatever the actual combination of causes, it appears that the critical energy and environmental crises will have to be more squarely faced by those we have called the children of Watergate than by today's mature adults. Except for the reality of third world famine, serious answers to these problems may be delayed; but eventually and in the not far distant future they must surely be faced.

The impending trials that may put the residual allegiance of Americans to an imminent test are those of a tormented economy: double-digit inflation, threatened collapse of the international monetary system, and depression. In 1974 inflation rose at a rate in excess of 12 percent; prime interest rates reached unprecedented levels; stock market averages plunged to depths that had been forgotten for fifteen years; and "free-floating" exchange rates in European money markets fluctuated with unnerving rapidity. Domestic analysts took little comfort from the indicators showing other Western nations in even more dire straits than the United States. Italy, it was widely agreed, was nearing bankruptcy; Japan and Great Britain were staggering under inflation rates of 25 and 20 percent a year. Outspoken leaders, ranging from the Finance Minister of West Germany to the President of France to the President of the World Bank, openly predicted global economic slump, depression, and widespread famine if current tendencies went unchecked. Secretary of State Henry Kissinger brooded to reporters that democracy as we have known it in this century cannot survive for more than three or four years at the current rate of inflation. If allowed to run its course, he predicted, inflation will result in economic, financial, and political anarchy—with authoritarian governments of the right or left. Western civilization will be transformed beyond the desires or imaginations of the leaders now in power.[35] Unfortunately, the causes of these conditions are unlikely to be affected by grand public exhortations or antiinflation lapel buttons.[36]

Since World War II, the United States has developed what economist Michael Tanzer terms "credit capitalism," in which business emphasis has increasingly been placed on the selling of credit.[37] In many instances, profits on credit have been more lucrative than on the underlying goods sold.[38] During the quarter century following the war, both consumer credit and mortgages increased by more than twentyfold, and since 1968 consumer credit jumped another 70 percent, standing at a record $187.4 billion in mid-1974. Expansionist monetary politics geared to provide liquidity in a chronically illiquid money market undoubtedly stimulated economic growth, but such policies stimulated the rate of inflation as well. According to Chase Manhattan Bank economist Eugene A. Birnbaum, "It is simply false to believe that the excessive expansion of credit is an inexpensive way to avert recession. Indeed, we are now learning how costly it really is, as inflation endangers the very existence of our economic system and political values." [39]

In October 1973 the Organization of Petroleum Exporting

155

Countries (OPEC) followed up the Arab oil boycott of Western nations with a unilateral increase in the price of oil. As 1973 ended, the price of a barrel of oil stood 400 percent higher than it had a year earlier. These dramatic events, coming at a time when U.S. dependency on OPEC countries for vital petroleum supplies was already great, and growing rapidly, placed another mammoth obstacle in the path of a solution to America's long-term balance-of-payments and balance-of-trade problems.[40] OPEC decisions held traumatic monetary consequences for the other oil-dependent industrial nations as well since the oil-energy deficit would undoubtedly aggravate international inflation. It is estimated that by July 1975 the foreign exchange holdings of the OPEC nations will be larger than those of all major industrial countries combined.[41] At the Ninth World Energy Conference in September 1974, President Gerald Ford warned: "Exorbitant [oil] prices can distort the world economy, run the risk of worldwide depression, and threaten the breakdown of world order and safety."

In the already unstable and weakening international monetary system that followed the multistage devaluation of the dollar and the eventual decision to enter the floating exchange rate system, the United States found itself in an intolerable dilemma in 1974: whether to attempt to withstand continued inflation at current levels and risk the collapse of what was left of the monetary system or to apply still additional deflationary pressures and potentially drive a recessionary cycle out of control and into irretrievable depression. Even an adroit attempt to escape these extremes threatened the possibility of both consequences at once. The *New York Times* gloomily reported that "certain parallels have been drawn between the current situation and the events that led to the Depression of the nineteen-thirties. The Wall Street crash of 1929 was followed by a European monetary collapse in 1931, precipitated by the failure of the Kreditanstalt of Vienna in July of that year. That in turn precipitated the 1933 crisis in

156

the United States." [42] In October 1974 a majority of Americans sampled by the Gallup organization said they thought another depression was soon to come.

The Democratic Prospect

The United States will not have another depression like that of the 1930s. Its population is increasingly alienated and divided. Its people have long ago given up their self-reliance and they have probably lost their resilience to adversity as well. We are, as a nation, the most pampered and profligate wastrels ever to exist, despoiling and destroying greater resources than some nations consume. Yet as a technologically powerful adversary, we are nonpareil. Attacked from without, we have a Maginot umbrella that could no doubt rain scorching destruction on the entire world. Attacked from within by economic dislocation and disorganization, we will most surely abandon our constitutional heritage in a matter of months or even weeks.

The American response to the severest loss of incomes, careers, and hopes in the 1930s was a model of orderliness. Aside from an almost pathetic Bonus Army march on Washington,[43] and the usual quotient of industrial strikes, the comparative resignation with which Americans accepted "everybody's tragedy as nobody's tragedy" stood in humble contrast to the street riots and violence, the ideological warfare, and the mass political upheavals elsewhere.[44] President Roosevelt is credited by historians as a "savior of capitalism." In the current mood of political alienation and matter-of-fact acceptance of violence, in a similarly depressed economy, it seems unlikely that even a Roosevelt could save the political and economic systems as we have known them.

The alienated Americans we have identified in this book are almost certainly those who would suffer first and most severely in a depressed economy. By and large, they are the blacks and

157

whites of the lower middle class. They already have the lowest incomes, the least education, and the largest relative burdens of consumer debt and government taxation. While the situation was similar in the past, the numbers and proportions are larger today. In addition, there is a greater self-awareness among this group of where they stand in American society. Eric Hoffer explains this self-awareness:

> . . . Now the American workingmen have indeed become
> a lesser breed of intellectuals and their attitude towards work
> fits Marx's description. They feel demeaned and dehumanized
> by the work they have to do, and see a job as a trap.
> Workingmen who have never read a book talk glibly about
> frustration, alienation, and relevance. Like intellectuals
> they expect a job not only to give them the wherewithal of
> living but to fill their lives with meaning.[45]

There is increasing concern even among the more success-ful that the whole American way of life is a fraud. Commenting on the younger members of this group, Paul Starr writes that "if [the system] collapsed, some might only congratulate them-selves that they had always known it would." [46]

Even if the present ministers and fiscal managers are able to solve or at least postpone the most immediate economic threats, and in the functional terms of daily existence, most of us do and must suppose this, the more serious, long-range chal-lenges of finite resources and international inequalities still lie ahead. At some point, society will have to change its premise: its economic and political life cannot be based on the "progress" of sustained growth. In the existing scheme of things, the alienated Americans appear less and less prepared for renewed allegiance: in time of troubles, they are the ones most likely to want and need change.

For those of us who retain a nostalgic attachment to the possibilities of postcapitalist pluralism, the decisions required to protect that polity—and required before a severe crisis descends—will seem radical and extreme. Radical choices favoring centralized planning, control of production and consumption, and other forms of resource management and use are essential for a transition to a stable, recycled economy. These seem improbable in our current version of representative democracy. Yet to stumble ahead clinging tenaciously to the past as a hope for the future is the most radical choice of all.

Appendix on Methods

TECHNICAL OPERATIONS for this book were conducted at Columbia University Computer Center (CUCC) in New York City. Computations were made on CUCC's IBM 360–91/360–75 using preestablished programs available in the Statistical Package for the Social Sciences (SPSS).*

The three national election study questions and answers that were used as indicators of *political distrust* were:

Do you think that quite a few of the people running the government are a little crooked, not very many are, or do you think hardly any of them are crooked at all?

1. Hardly any (0)
2. Not many (0)
3. Quite a lot (1)
4. Don't know (DK) (8)
5. No answer (NA) (8)

How much of the time do you think you can trust the government in Washington to do what is right—just about always, most of the time, or only some of the time?

1. Always (0)
2. Most of the time (0)

* See Norman H. Nie, Dale H. Bent, and C. Hadlai Hule, *SPSS: Statistical Package for the Social Sciences* (New York: McGraw-Hill, 1970).

3. Some of the time (1)
4. None of the time (volunteered response) (1)
5. DK (8)
6. NA (8)

Would you say that the government is pretty much run by a few big interests looking out for themselves or that it is run for the benefit of all people?

1. For benefit of all (0)
2. For few big interests (1)
3. Other; depends (1)
4. DK (8)
5. NA (8)

The responses to these questions were scored "0" for an "integrated" or "allegiant" response, "1" for an "alienated" response, or "8" for missing data. For example, when respondents were asked how many of the people running the government they thought were "a little crooked," the responses "hardly any" and "not many" were scored "0" (allegiant); the response "quite a lot" was scored "1" (alienated); and DK and NA were scored "8" (missing data). An "extremely distrustful" respondent was one who scored "3," one point for each question.

Three additional indicators were used to measure *political powerlessness*. First, members of the sample were told, "Now I'd like to read some of the kinds of things people tell us when we interview them. I'll read them one at a time and you just tell me whether you agree or disagree":

People like me don't have any say about what the government does.

1. Agree (1)
2. Disagree (0)
3. DK (8)
4. NA (8)

Sometimes politics and government seem so complicated that a person like me can't really understand what's going on.

1. Agree (1)
2. Disagree (0)
3. DK (8)
4. NA (8)

I don't think public officials care much what people like me think.

1. Agree (1)
2. Disagree (0)
3. DK (8)
4. NA (8)

The following questions and responses comprised the scale of *political meaninglessness:*

Who do you think would be most likely to do what you want on the (most important problem to be faced by the country), the Democrats, the Republicans, or wouldn't there be any difference?

1. Democrats (0)
2. No difference (1)
3. Republicans (0)
4. DK (1)
5. NA (8)

Who do you think would be most likely to do what you want on the (second most important problem to be faced by the country), the Democrats, the Republicans, or wouldn't there by any difference?

1. Democrats (0)
2. No difference (1)
3. Republicans (0)
4. DK (1)
5. NA (8)

Do you think it will make any difference in how you and

your family get along financially whether the Republicans or Democrats win the election?

1. Very important differences. Many differences. Big difference (mentions 3 or more differences) (0)
2. Important differences. Some differences, NA what. (mentions 1 or 2 differences) (0)
3. Minor differences. Not important. Some differences but DK what they are (0)
4. No differences. Not important. About the same (1)
5. Depends; Other (8)
6. DK (8)
7. NA (8)

As with the scale of political distrust above, the answers to questions about political powerlessness and meaninglessness were scored "0" (allegiant), "1" (alienated), or "8" (missing data). Scored in this manner, each set of questions forms the Guttman Scale that is described in a simplified fashion in note 24 of chapter 1.* As indicated, the items in the scale must constitute an ordered set of responses; they are related to one another and they are cumulative. Substantial inconsistencies or "errors" in this order indicate that the items are measuring something other than one dimension. No matter how the nine items of the three different scales are ordered, they will not form a consistent, single Guttman Scale of political alienation.

The consistency (unidimensionality) of a Guttman Scale is checked with the use of a simple formula known as the *coefficient of reproducibility* (CR):

$$CR = 1.00 - (e/r)$$

* Additional discussion of Guttman scaling is found in Oliver Benson, *Political Science Laboratory* (Columbus, Ohio: Merrill, 1969), pp. 240–244; Louis Guttman, "A Basis for Scaling Qualitative Data," *American Sociological Review*, 9 (April 1944), 139–150; Louis Guttman, "An Outline of Some New Methodology in Social Research," *Public Opinion Quarterly*, 18 (Winter 1954–1955), 395–404; Nie, *et al., SPSS*, pp. 196–203.

Where: e = errors and r = responses. In its strictest terms, the scale requires ten items and a CR of .90 or greater. However, these are arbitrary limits, chosen by Guttman, to insure a high level of validity for psychological testing. Other social and political researchers have modified these requirements especially when, as in this study, the choice of indicators is limited by the data available. Here the number of indicators in each scale is three, and the CR for each of the scales varied between 0.86 and 0.95. Thus, we speak of each scale as "approximating" the Guttman Scale.

The items in our three scales do not form a single reliable Guttman Scale, but they were strongly interrelated in every survey. This association of indicators and the history of the concept of political alienation suggest the desirability of creating a multidimensional composite scale from the nine indicators. Assuming that each question has an equal value, the responses were simply added. A respondent who gave alienated answers to all nine questions scored a "9"; the respondent who gave all allegiant answers scored "0." On the combined scale, total scores of "0," "1," and "2," were designated "allegiant," and those totalling "7," "8," and "9" were termed "extremely alienated." The middle-range score, "3" through "6," identified the mixed responses sometimes referred to in the study as "disillusioned." These categories are arbitrary, but the assumption is that the respondent who made alienated replies on all three scales must surely feel a deep sense of estrangement from his government. This, of course, is a requirement for the "extremely alienated" category used throughout the book.

The items that formed the *political apathy* scale are the following:

Generally speaking, would you say that you personally care a good deal which party wins the presidential election this fall or that you don't care very much which party wins?

1. Care very much (0)
2. Care, care pretty much (0)
3. Pro-con, depends (0)
4. Don't care very much, care a little, care some (1)
5. Don't care at all (1)
6. Don't care about party, only about the man (0)
7. DK (1)
8. NA (8)

Some people don't pay too much attention to election campaigns. How about you—were you very interested in this campaign, fairly interested, just slightly interested, or not interested at all in it?

1. Very interested (0)
2. Fairly interested (0)
3. Slightly interested (0)
4. Not at all interested (1)
5. NA (8)

Some people seem to follow what's going on in government and public affairs most of the time whether there's an election going on or not. Others aren't that interested. Would you say you follow what's going on in government and public affairs most of the time, some of the time, only now and then, or hardly at all?

1. All the time (0)
2. Some of the time (0)
3. Only now and then (1)
4. Hardly at all (1)
5. NA (8)

On the apathy scale, politically interested responses were scored "0"; apathetic responses were scored "1"; and missing data was scored "8," as indicated in the parentheses following each response. The three indicators of political apathy consistently approximated a Guttman Scale with a CR of greater than 0.90.

Notes

Chapter 1

1. The term "alienation" originates from the Latin noun *alienato*, which comes from the verb *alienare* (to make something another, to take away, to remove). See Richard Schacht, *Alienation*, with an introductory essay by Walter Kaufmann (Garden City, N.Y.: Anchor Books, 1971), pp. 9–14. For other works on the linguistic and intellectual background of the term "alienation," see G. W. F. Hegel, "On Christianity," in *Early Theological Writings*, T. M. Knox and Richard Kroner, trans. (New York: Harper, 1948); G. W. F. Hegel, *Lectures on the History of Philosophy*, J. Sibree, trans. (New York: Dover Books, 1956), P. 3, Sec. 3, Chap. 2; Lewis Feuer, "What Is Alienation? The Career of a Concept," *New Politics*, 1, no. 3 (Spring 1962), 116–134; Frank Johnson (ed.), *Alienation: Concept, Term, and Meaning* (New York: Seminar Press, 1973); Irving Howwitz, "On Alienation and the Social Order," *Philosophy and Phenomenological Research*, 27, no. 2 (1966), 230–237; Helen B. Lamb and N. S. Lehrman, "On Alienation: Two Contrasting Views," *Science and Society*, 25 (1961), 260–269; Herbert H. Stroup, "Historical Explanation of Alienation," *Social Casework*, 42 (March 1961), 107–111.

2. Jean Jacques Rousseau, *The Political Writings of Jean Jacques Rousseau*, C. E. Vaugh (ed.), 3 vols. (Cambridge, Eng.: The University Press, 1915).

3. Jean Jacques Rousseau, *The First and Second Discourses on the Origin of Inequality* (New York: St. Martin's Press, 1964), p. 178.

4. See B. Baczko, "Rousseau et l'alienation sociale," *Annales J. J. Rousseau*, 35 (1963), 223–237.

5. Rousseau, *The Social Contract*, G. D. H. Cole, trans. (New York: Dutton, 1950), p. 3.

166

6. Rousseau's concept of alienation as the "transmission" of man's natural rights to the community and his resulting "detachment" is similar to the way *alienation* was used in theories of natural law, contemporary definitions of *alienation* in real property law, and *alienation of affections* in domestic relations law.

7. For further discussion of Smith's use of the concept of alienation, see Robert Lamb, "Adam Smith's Concept of Alienation," *Oxford Economic Papers,* 25, no. 2 (July 1973), 275–285; Ronald L. Meek (ed.) "The Scottish Contribution to Marxist Sociology," in *Economics and Ideology and Other Essays: Studies in the Development of Economic Thought* (London: Chapman & Hall, 1967), pp. 34–50; Fritz Pappenheim, *The Alienation of Modern Man* (New York: Monthly Review Press, 1959), pp. 82–84; E. G. West, "The Political Economy of Alienation, Karl Marx and Adam Smith," *Oxford Economic Papers,* 21, no. 1 (March 1969), 1–23.

8. Adam Smith, *An Inquiry into the Nature and Causes of the Wealth of Nations,* Edwin Cannan, ed. (London: Methuen, 1960), vol. 2, pp. 303–304.

9. *Ibid.*

10. *Ibid.*

11. For Hegel's own discussion of alienation (*Entfremdung*), see G. W. F. Hegel *The Phenomenology of Mind,* J. B. Baille, trans. (New York: Harper & Row, 1967); G. W. F. Hegel, *Philosophy of Right,* T. M. Knox, trans. (New York: Clarendon Press, 1942). For further commentary, see Shlomo Avineri, *Hegel's Theory of the Modern State* (New York: Cambridge University Press, 1972), pp. 90–98; Jean Hippolite, *Studies on Hegel and Marx,* John O'Neill, trans. (New York: Harper & Row, 1973); Walter Kaufmann, *Hegel: Reinterpretation, Texts, and Commentary* (Garden City, N.Y.: Doubleday, 1965).

12. Karl Marx, *Economic and Philosophic Manuscripts of 1844,* T. B. Bottomore, trans., in Erich Fromm, *Marx's Concept of Man* (New York: F. Ungar, 1971). For additional commentary, see Bertell Ollman, *Alienation: Marx's Conception of Man in Capitalist Society* (Cambridge, Eng.: The University Press, 1971), and Joachim Israel, *Alienation: From Marx to Modern Sociology* (Boston: Allyn and Bacon, 1971). Other useful sources on Marx's theory of alienation include Herbert Aptheker, *Marxism and Alienation: A Symposium* (New York: Humanities Press, 1965); Shlomo Avineri, *The Social and Political Thought of Karl Marx* (Cambridge, Eng.: The University Press, 1969); Erich Fromm (ed.), *Social Humanism* (Garden City, N.Y.: Doubleday, 1966); Lewis S. Feuer, *Marx and the In-*

tellectuals (Garden City, N.Y.: Doubleday, 1969); Georg Lukacs, *History and Class Consciousness* (Cambridge, Mass.: MIT Press, 1971); E. Mandel and K. Novack, *The Marxist Theory of Alienation* (New York: Pathfinder, 1973); Istvan Meszaros, *Marx's Theory of Alienation*, 3rd ed. (New York: Harper & Row, 1972); Daniel Bell, "The Rediscovery of Alienation: Some Notes Along the Quest for the Historical Marx," *Journal of Philosophy*, 56 (November 1959), 933–952.

13. Karl Marx, *Economic and Philosophic Manuscripts of 1844* (Moscow, USSR: Foreign Languages Publishing House, 1961), p. 69.

14. Karl Marx and Friedrich Engels, "The Communist Manifesto," *Marx-Engels: Selected Works* (Moscow, USSR: Foreign Languages Publishing House, 1954), vol. 1, p. 54.

15. See James Joll, *The Anarchists* (Boston: Little, Brown, 1965); James Joll and David E. Apter (eds.), *Anarchism Today* (Garden City, N.Y.: Doubleday, 1971); George Woodcock, *Anarchism: A History of Libertarian Movements* (New York: Meridian, 1962); John D. Hicks, *The Populist Revolt* (Minneapolis, Minn.: University of Minnesota Press, 1955); Richard Hofstadter, *The Age of Reform* (New York: Vintage, 1960), Chaps. 1, 2; Harold V. Raoder, *Utopia in American Political Thought* (Tuscon: University of Arizona Press, 1967); Peyton E. Richter, *Utopias: Social Ideals and Communal Experiments* (Boston: Holbrook Press, 1971); Frank E. Manuel (ed.), *Utopias and Utopian Thought* (Boston: Beacon Press, 1967); Benjamin Zablocki, *The Joyful Community* (Baltimore, Md.: Penguin, 1971); Richard Fairfield, *Communes USA* (Baltimore: Penguin, 1972); Keith Melville, *Communes in the Counter Culture* (New York: William Morrow, 1972); Ron E. Roberts, *The New Communes* (Englewood Cliffs, N.J.: Prentice-Hall, 1971); Dan Leon, *The Kibbutz: A New Way of Life* (New York: Pergamon, 1969); Medfus E. Spiro, *Kibbutz: Venture in Utopia* (New York: Schocken, 1971).

16. See, for example, Émile Durkheim, *The Division of Labor in Society*, G. Simpson, trans. (New York: Free Press, 1964); Lewis S. Feuer, "What Is Alienation? The Career of a Concept," in Maurice R. Stein and Arthur J. Vidich (eds.), *Sociology on Trial* (Englewood Cliffs, N.J.: Prentice-Hall, 1965); Dwight Dean, "Alienation: Its Meaning and Measurement," *American Sociological Review*, 26 (1961), 753–758; Melvin Seeman, "On the Meaning of Alienation," *American Sociological Review*, 24 (December 1959), 783–791; Arthur G. Neal and Solomon Rettig, "Dimensions of Alienation among Manual and Non-Manual Workers," *American Sociological Review*,

28 (August 1963), 599–608; and Kenneth Kenniston, *The Uncommitted: Alienated Youth in American Society* (New York: Dell, 1965). See also Arthur H. Miller, "Political Issues and Trust in Government: 1964–1972," paper prepared for delivery at the American Political Science Association Annual Meeting, Washington, D.C., September 5–9, 1972.

17. See especially Angus Campbell, Philip E. Converse, Warren E. Miller, and Donald F. Stokes, *The American Voter* (New York: Wiley, 1960); Robert E. Lane, *Political Ideology* (New York: Free Press, 1962); Robert E. Agger, Marshall N. Goldstein, and Stanley A. Pearl, "Political Cynicism: Measurement and Meaning," *Journal of Politics*, 23 (August 1961), 477–506; Joel Aberbach, "Alienation and Political Behavior," *American Political Science Review*, 58 (March 1969), 86–99; and Edgar Litt, "Political Cynicism and Political Futility," *Journal of Politics*, 25 (May 1963), 312–323.

18. Ada W. Finifter, "Dimensions of Political Alienation," *American Political Science Review*, 64 (June 1970), 389–410.

19. *Ibid.*, pp. 389–391.

20. From the international surveys conducted by Gabriel Almond and Sidney Verba, *The Civic Culture* (Princeton, N.J.: Princeton University Press, 1963), Finifter selected for examination "twenty six questions whose manifest content was judged related to the political alienation domain. . . ." *Ibid.*, p. 391. These were subjected to both factor analysis and item analysis techniques in order to uncover latent dimensionality among the multiple items. Finifter's specific method is summarized *ibid.*, pp. 393–395.

21. The illusiveness of "alienation" as an empirical concept in contemporary commentary is aptly described by Kenneth Kenniston: "The ambiguous concept of alienation has in recent years become increasingly fashionable and, partly as a result, increasingly devoid of any specific meaning. . . . [It is a] rhetorical, [and] at times emotive concept." *The Uncommitted*, p. 449.

22. The *Digest* predicted 32 states for Landon with 370 electoral votes against 16 states and 161 electoral votes for Roosevelt. On election day, 1936, Roosevelt outpolled Landon 27,476,673 votes to 16,679,583, winning electoral votes from all but 2 states (Maine and Vermont). Arthur M. Schlesinger, Jr., *The Politics of Upheaval* (Boston: Houghton Mifflin, 1960), pp. 639–642.

23. A basic explanation of the Guttman Scale is found in Louis Guttman, "A Basis for Scaling Qualitative Data," *American Sociological Review*, 9 (April 1944), 139–150. Further discussions of this tech-

nique are found in Guttman, "An Outline of Some New Methodology in Social Research," *Public Opinion Quarterly,* 18 (Winter 1954-1955), 395–404, and Edward Suchman, "The Logic of Scale Construction," *Educational and Psychological Measurement,* 10 (Spring 1950), 79–93.

24. H. Douglas Price points out that the Guttman Scale "is simply a test of whether a series of criteria can be so arranged as to result in cumulative divisions of the population under study." Using the example of a "population" of buildings in New York City, Price suggests that if we had no quantitative concept such as the meter or inch, we could classify all buildings on Manhattan as to whether they were at least as tall as the following examples:

Bldg. Classes	As high as			Not as high as		
	Empire State Bldg.	Chrysler Bldg.	Guggenheim Museum	Empire State Bldg.	Chrysler Bldg.	Guggenheim Museum
Type I	X	X	X			
Type II			X	X	X	
Type III			X	X	X	
Type IV				X	X	X

This is a perfect Guttman-type scale of buildings that is based on a series of qualitative distinctions: "The result is a ranking of buildings which are either 'more' or 'less' high than certain others, but without any connotations of cardinal measurement. Thus the differences in height between the Empire State Building and Chrysler Building are not the same as that between the Chrysler Building and the Guggenheim Museum." H. Douglas Price, "Are Southern Democrats Different? An Application of Scale Analysis to Senate Voting Patterns," in Nelson W. Polsby, Robert A. Dentler, and Paul A. Smith (eds.), *Politics and Social Life* (Boston: Houghton Mifflin, 1963), pp. 743–744. Of course, there are far better measures for dealing with buildings and other physical phenomena, but for attitudes and other nonordinal, qualitative expressions, the Guttman Scale is one of the best measuring tools available.

25. There was some erosion of normally strong black support for the national Democratic ticket during the Eisenhower candidacies, especially in 1956, but blacks returned to support John Kennedy in large

numbers. In 1964, during the Johnson-Goldwater contest, blacks voted for Johnson in numbers exceeding 95 percent of their total national vote and better than 99 percent in many urban areas. These percentages have not been repeated, but black allegiance to Democratic candidates remains quite high.

26. The sense of importance in the 1964 election outcome was widely felt despite the fact that actual voter turnout as a percentage of those eligible declined slightly from the high (63.8 percent) of 1960. Theodore White reports:

> For thirty years Republicans and Democrats had fought each other in the arena of the center, where their differences, though real, were small, narrow or administrative. . . . Goldwater, however, proposed to give the nation a choice, not an echo— and not just one choice but a whole series of choices, a whole system of ideas which clashed with the governing ideas that had ruled America for a generation: a choice on nuclear weapons, a choice on defense posture, a choice on the treatment of Negroes, a choice on dealing with Communism, a choice on the nature of central government. *The Making of the President: 1964* (New York: Atheneum, 1965), p. 295.

Chapter 2

1. As late as 1964, only 24 of the 228 Arkansas school districts educating both blacks and whites had any integrated classrooms whatever; 0.811 percent of the black school population attended schools with whites. In the entire South in 1964, only 2.14 percent of black school children attended integrated schools. *A Statistical Summary, State by State, of School Segregation-Desegregation in the Southern and Border Area from 1954 to the Present*, 15th rev. (Nashville, Tenn.: Southern Education Reporting Service, 1965).

2. An autobiographical account of this migration north from the Deep South is superbly told in Richard Wright's classic *Black Boy* (New York: Harper, 1945). An excellent case study of the impact of the movement in its final stages in Chicago has been written by St. Clair Drake and Horace R. Cayton, *Black Metropolis: A Study of Negro Life in a Northern City*, 2 vols. (New York: Harper & Row, 1962). See also George W. Groh, *The Black Migration: The Journey to Urban America* (New York: McKay, 1972).

3. Recent studies of black alienation include Bonnie Bullough, "Alienation in the Ghetto," *American Journal of Sociology*, 72 (March 1967), 469–478; Russell Middleton, "Alienation, Race, and Education," *American Sociological Review*, 28 (December 1963), 973–977; H. Edward Ransford, "Isolation, Powerlessness, and Violence," *American Journal of Sociology*, 73 (March 1968), 581–591; and Sumati N. Dubey and Morris L. Grant, "Powerlessness Among Disadvantaged Blacks," *Social Casework*, 51 (May 1970), 285–290.

4. Support of Black Americans for an Independent Black Political Party by Degree of Political Alienation—1972 (in percentages)

Support for Black Political Party	Black Americans Degree of Alienation		
	Allegiance	Disillusionment	Alienation
Would Support	28.6	30.9	52.4
Support Depends on Circumstances	28.6	41.8	23.8
Would Not Support	42.9	27.8	23.8
Total *	100.1	100.5	100.0
	(7)	(55)	(21)

* Percentages over 100 are the result of rounding error.

5. The feelings expressed by Ralph and Joyce White and others we interviewed in similar situations are in tune with the outrage expressed repeatedly by the subjects of Peter Binzen's *Whitetown USA* (New York: Vintage, 1971). As Binzen pointedly notes, "In the 1968 Presidential election, many Whitetowners voted not for Nixon but for George Wallace. They helped the Alabama segregationist pile up nine million votes." *Ibid.*, p. 11. Other useful sources on Americans like the Whites include Richard M. Scammon and Ben J. Wattenberg, *The Real Majority* (New York: Coward, McCann & Geoghegan, 1971); Louise Kapp Howe (ed.), *The White Majority* (New York: Vintage, 1970); and Seymour Martin Lipset and Earl Raab, *The Politics of Unreason* (New York: Harper & Row, 1970).

6. In 1972, 42 percent of the alienated Americans, like Ralph and Joyce, admitted that they had not voted in the presidential election.

7. Richard Nixon's equivocation in 1960 in deciding "which he

wanted, the Northern Negro or Southern white vote . . ." was not to be repeated in 1968. With experience behind them, Nixon strategists, most notably Kevin P. Phillips, *The Emerging Republican Majority* (Garden City, N.Y.: Doubleday, 1970), moved in aggressively and profitably on the southern electoral count.

8. Many thousands of southern blacks were still disfranchised in 1960, and those who could vote were divided in their party loyalties. Even among the leadership of the emerging civil rights movement, there remained considerable attachment to Eisenhower Republicanism. The father of Dr. Martin Luther King, for example, came out for Nixon, based on religious grounds. In the closing weeks of the campaign, the Kennedys' intervention to secure Dr. King's release from prison caused the elder Reverend King to abruptly change his mind: "Because this man was willing to wipe the tears from my daughter[in-law]'s eyes, I've got a suitcase of votes, and I'm going to take them to Mr. Kennedy and dump them in his lap." Quoted in Theodore H. White, *The Making of the President: 1960* (New York: Atheneum, 1962), p. 323.

9. See David M. Chalmers, *Hooded Americanism* (Garden City, N.Y.: Doubleday, 1965), chap. 47.

10. Governor Wallace was also capitalizing on the growing distain and resentment of the American workingman for his educated "betters." Here Wallace's repeated refrain hit dead center: "And we are going to show them in November that the average American is sick and tired of all those over-educated ivory-tower folks with pointed heads looking down their noses at us." Ben A. Franklin, "Politics: Wallace Finds Attack on the Press and TV Is a Successful Campaign Tactic," *New York Times*, September 3, 1968.

11. Quoted in Peter Schrag, "The Forgotten American," *Harper's Magazine*, 239 (August 1969), 28.

12. *Ibid.*, p. 27.

13. Gabriel A. Almond and Sidney Verba, *The Civic Culture: Political Attitudes and Democracy in Five Nations* (Princeton, N.J.: Princeton University Press, 1963), pp. 80–81. See also Robert Blanner, *Alienation and Freedom: The Factory Worker and His Industry* (Chicago: University of Chicago Press, 1964); Arthur G. Neal and Salmon Rettig, "Dimensions of Alienation Among Manual and Non-manual Workers," *American Sociological Review*, 28 (August 1963), 599–608; and Leonard Pearlin, "Alienation from Work," *American Sociological Review*, 27 (June 1962), 314–326.

14. Support for the traditional view may be found in Robert E. Agger, Marshall Goldstein, and Stanley Pearl, "Political Cynicism: Measurement and Meaning," *Journal of Politics,* 23 (August 1961), 477–506; William Erbe, "Social Involvement and Political Activity," *American Sociological Review,* 19 (April 1964), 198–215.

15. Though somewhat less articulate than many of Kenneth Keniston's respondents at Yale College, Sherman Woods is in many respects quite typical of the "alienated youth in American society" whom Keniston so well describes in *The Uncommitted: Alienated Youth in American Society* (New York: Dell, 1960).

16. Probably the most influential philosophic voices speaking the feelings and needs of Sherman and Tricia Woods and others like them were those of two alienated activists from another era, Helen and Scott Nearing, *Living the Good Life: How to Live Sanely and Simply in a Troubled World* (New York: Schocken, 1970); also Scott Nearing, *The Making of a Radical* (New York: Harper & Row, 1972).

17. Most laterday activists and kindred spirits might probably agree with the definition of "the movement" offered by Mitchell Goodman, which is rendered here in part:

The essential experience of the Movement is a willingness to live under the burden of change, to carry it and to articulate it. . . . Painfully, with their bodies, their feelings, as well as their minds.

We live in confusion verging on chaos in the midst of a process of change we barely understand . . . a world in which there is no predictable future, in which governments offer control and terror in place of the "pursuit of happiness." A world in which war criminals are called leaders. . . .

The Movement has a life of its own—a complex, dynamic way of speaking and thinking and acting that makes it like nothing else that has happened in America. It began with racism and war. It is an ongoing revelation. . . . (We are not yet in revolution; we are in movement toward it, trying to get ready for it.) . . . *The Movement Toward a New America* (New York: Knopf, 1970), pp. vi-viii.

18. On May 17, 1968, Daniel and Philip Berrigan and seven others invaded the office of Local (draft) Board 33 in Catonsville, Maryland. The arrest, trial, and conviction of the Berrigans and the antiwar struggle they led are probably best chronicalled in William VanEtten Casey (ed.), *The Berrigans* (New York: Avon, 1971).

Chapter 3

1. Whenever we talked with people in their thirties and early forties, the memory of President Kennedy's assassination was acute and painful. Trivial details of that day in their lives were recalled vividly. For most, the assassination was a landmark in time, and for many, it was the watershed of their current thinking about politics.

2. In 1970 more than 64 percent of American working women were employed as domestic servants or as service, sales, or clerical personnel. In contrast, some 70 percent of men working were employed as professional and technical workers, managers or proprietors, craftsmen, foremen, or factory workers. All these male-dominated jobs are more highly paid than those generally designated for women. "Rebelling Women—The Reason," *U.S. News and World Report* (April 13, 1970), p. 35.

3. Good summaries of discriminating practices used against women are found in Joan Jordan, *The Place of American Women* (Boston: New England Free Press, 1969), and Cynthia Fuchs Epstein, *Women's Place* (Berkeley: University of California Press, 1970).

4. Surprisingly little serious political analysis of women's attitudes and behavior has yet been published. One notable exception is Kirsten Amundsen, *The Silenced Majority: Women and American Democracy* (Englewood Cliffs, N.J.: Prentice-Hall, 1971).

5. John's economic failure, his social isolation, and his political alienation, in combination, are not untypical of others for whom success was much desired and never grasped. See Michael Aiken, *et al., Economic Failure, Alienation and Extremism* (Ann Arbor: University of Michigan Press, 1968).

6. Lipset and Raab found that, both North and South, larger proportions of Goldwater supporters than Johnson supporters voted for Wallace. Wallace did even better among southern voters who had supported Goldwater in 1964. The explanation for this is that Wallace was most popular among "independents" and habitual nonvoters, such as John Shearworth, and there were proportionately more people in both of these categories in the South than in the North. For example, almost half of the 1964 southern nonvoters who voted in 1968 voted for Wallace. Seymour Martin Lipset and Earl Raab, *The Politics of Unreason* (New York: Harper & Row, 1970), pp. 378–387. Lipset and Raab also found that urban manual workers were more likely to be pro-Wallace than were those in the nonmanual middle class. Even among Goldwater supporters, most white-collar workers found Wallace objectionable. *Ibid,* p. 361.

7. Sociological studies of the alienating experience of separation and divorce include Nathan Ackerman, "Divorce and Alienation," *Mental Hygiene,* 43 (1959), 118–126, and Florence Rosenstock and Bernard Kutner, "Alienation and Family Crisis," *Sociological Quarterly,* 8 (Summer 1967), 397–405. The special situation of black veterans is treated by James M. Fendrich and L. J. Axelson, "Marital Status and Political Alienation among Black Veterans," *American Journal of Sociology,* 77 (September 1971), 245–261.

8. Surprisingly little study has been done of widowhood. Perhaps the best personal account of the impact of losing a spouse is that by Lynn Caine, *Widow* (New York: Morrow, 1974).

9. Other researchers have uncovered this relationship in the past, noting also that older age is associated with cynicism and alienation, independent of the fact that contemporary youth tends to have experienced more years of formal education than have the elderly. Robert E. Agger, Marshall Goldstein, and Stanley Pearl, "Political Cynicism: Measurement and Meaning," *Journal of Politics,* 23 (August 1961), 477–506, and Arthur Kornhauser, Albert J. Mayer, and Harold Sheppard, *When Labor Votes* (New York: University Books, 1956).

10. Kenneth Keniston, *The Uncommitted: Alienated Youth in American Society* (New York: Dell, 1965); Kenneth Keniston, *Youth and Dissent: The Rise of a New Opposition* (New York: Harcourt, Brace, Jovanovich, 1971); Paul Goodman, *Growing Up Absurd* (New York: Knopf, 1960). See also Charles A. Reich, *The Greening of America* (New York: Random House, 1970); Theodore Roszak, *The Making of a Counter Culture* (Garden City, N.Y.: Doubleday, 1969); Seymour L. Halleck, "Psychiatric Treatment of the Alienated College Student," *American Journal of Psychiatry* (November 1967), pp. 642–650; and Steven Kelman, "These Are Three of the Alienated," *New York Times Magazine* (October 22, 1967), pp. 39, 140, 142–148.

11. Noteworthy accounts of these demonstrations include Jerry L. Avorn and Robert Friedman, *Up Against the Ivy Wall* (New York: Atheneum, 1969); James Simon Kunen, *The Strawberry Statement: Notes of a College Revolutionary* (New York: Random House, 1968); Norman Mailer, *Miami and the Siege of Chicago* (New York: New American Library, 1971); and Ken Hurwitz, *Marching Nowhere* (New York: Norton, 1971).

12. Charles A. Reich, *The Greening of America,* Peter L. Berger and Brigitte Berger, "The Blueing of America," *The New Republic,* 164 (April 3, 1971), 20–23.

13. In late 1973, Congress passed a bill to boost Social Security

benefits by 7 percent in March 1974, followed by an additional 4 percent increase in June 1974. The wage base subject to Social Security tax was also increased—to $13,200, for a maximum tax of $772.20 per year. The 1973 legislation also raised initial benefits to be paid by the federal Supplemental Security Income (SSI) program.

Chapter 4

1. Nearly twenty years ago, William H. White pointed out that "the organization man" is a mover in the literal sense. "Almost by definition, the organization man is a man who left home and, as it was said of the man who went from the Midwest to Harvard, kept on going. There have always been people who left home, and the number of them is not decreasing but increasing—and so greatly that those who stay put in the home town are often as affected by the emigration as those who leave." *The Organization Man* (New York: Simon and Schuster, 1956), p. 269.

2. Vance Packard, *A Nation of Strangers* (New York: McKay, 1972), p. vii.

3. *Ibid.*, pp. 6–7.

4. Atlas Van Lines estimated that more than half of the many million changes of address each year are the results of corporate transfers or changes of jobs. A United Van Lines spokesman attributed the acceleration of long-distance moving in recent years largely to the transfer of top- and middle-management personnel by major companies. *Ibid.*, p. 19. William White received similar estimates of the importance of corporate transfers to geographic mobility in the mid-1950s. White, *The Organization Man*, p. 270.

5. C. Wright Mills argued that the independent entrepreneur model, once dominant in the nineteenth century, has lost most of its importance with this century's large-scale organizational dominance:

> The free entrepreneurs of the old middle classes have diminished
> as a proportion of the gainfully occupied. They no longer enjoy
> the social position they once held. They no longer fulfill their
> classic role as integrators of the social structure in which they live
> and work. These are the indices of their decline. The causes of
> that decline involve the whole push and shove of modern industrial
> society. . . . *White Collar* (New York: Oxford University
> Press, 1956), p. 13.

Nonetheless, physicians, lawyers, and other professionals who have retained a small-business orientation continue to rank high in occupational prestige polls. And the "pillars" of small town societies have yet to be dominated by international conglomerate branch managers.

6. Analysis of the national election surveys consistently showed no relationship between divorce, after the period of separation, and political alienation.

7. Numerous studies have found that persons of higher socioeconomic status are less likely to develop cynical attitudes toward politics. See Robert E. Agger, Marshall Goldstein, and Stanley Pearl, "Political Cynicism: Measurement and Meaning," *Journal of Politics,* 23 (August 1961), 477–506; Gabriel Almond and Sidney Verba, *The Civic Culture* (Princeton, N.J.: Princeton University Press, 1963); William Erbe, "Social Involvement and Political Activity," *American Sociological Review,* 19 (April 1964), 198–215; Arthur Kornhauser, Albert J. Mayer, and Harold Sheppard, *When Labor Votes* (New York: University Books, 1956). See also Joel I. Nelson, "Participation and Integration: The Case of the Small Businessman," *American Sociological Review,* 33 (June 1968), 427–438.

8. See Agger, *et al.,* "Political Cynicism," and Kornhauser, *et. al., When Labor Votes.*

9. Lower-echelon white-collar bureaucrats, however, are likely to feel considerably more estranged from their jobs and surroundings than Arnold. See Victor A. Gelineau, "The White Collar Supervisor: Job Identification and Alienation" (unpublished Ph.D. dissertation, Columbia University, 1966); George A. Miller, "Professionals in Bureaucracy: Alienation Among Industrial Scientists and Engineers," *American Sociological Review,* 32 (October 1967), 755–767; Jon M. Shepard, *Automation and Alienation: A Study of the Office and Factory Worker* (Cambridge, Mass.: MIT Press, 1971); and Mills, *White Collar.*

10. As a percentage of the population, not many people of any political persuasion attend political gatherings. Only about 10 percent attended any political meetings whatever in 1972.

11. Numerous studies have shown that those who have strong party preferences, such as Arnold and Byron, are more likely to have an active interest in the political process and to proselytize to others as well. See Bernard R. Berelson, Paul F. Lazarsfeld, and William N. McPhee, *Voting* (Chicago: University of Chicago Press, 1954); Angus Campbell, Gerald Gurin, and Warren Miller, *The Voter Decides* (Evanston, Ill.: Row, Peterson, 1954); and Angus Campbell, Philip

Converse, Warren Miller, and Donald Stokes, *The American Voter* (New York: Wiley, 1960).

12. Like Arnold, the still allegiant Americans in 1972 were far more likely than those who had become alienated to attach bumper stickers to their cars, don political lapel buttons, and donate to a political party or candidate. Slightly over 20 percent of the allegiant group became involved in each of these areas of political participation in 1972.

13. In 1967 more than half of those who had an opinion (42 percent) agreed with Arnold and the proposition, "The government has gone too far in regulating business and interfering with the free enterprise system." At the same time, 43 percent said that they would like to see large business corporations have less influence in America. See Lloyd A. Free and Hadley Cantril, *The Political Beliefs of Americans: A Study of Public Opinion* (New York: Simon and Schuster, 1968).

14. In the face of overwhelming congressional sentiment favoring his impeachment and conviction for "high crimes and misdemeanors," President Richard M. Nixon resigned his office, August 8, 1974.

15. As Democratic governor of South Carolina in 1948, J. Strom Thurmond led a southern revolt against President Harry Truman and the northern-dominated Democratic Party. Thurmond's "Dixiecrats," with their firm state's rights platform, polled nearly 1.2 million popular votes and 39 electoral votes in the presidential election. The best brief account of the Dixiecrat movement is found in V. O. Key, Jr., *Southern Politics in State and Nation* (New York: Knopf, 1950), pp. 329–344. In 1964, as a second-term U.S. senator, Thurmond switched from the Democratic to the Republican Party.

16. The term "anomie" originated with Émile Durkheim and has since been used by many other social scientists. Anomie embraces a host of individual feelings, including ineffectiveness, a lack of values and direction, and the sense that authority figures no longer care. Robert E. Lane, *Political Life* (Glencoe, Ill.: Free Press, 1959), pp. 166–169.

17. Any number of social commentators have painted stark portraits of these modern American social patterns. Charles Reich, for example, sees America as:

. . . one vast, terrifying anticommunity. The great organizations to which most people give their working day, and the apartments and suburbs to which they return at night, are equally places of loneliness and alienation. Modern living has obliterated place, locality, and neighborhood, and given us the anonymous separateness of our existence. The family, the most basic social system, has been ruthlessly stripped to its functional essentials. Friendship has been coated over with a layer of impenetrable artificiality as men strive to live roles designed for them. Protocol, competition, hostility, and fear have replaced the warmth of the circle of affection which might sustain man against a hostile universe. *The Greening of America* (New York: Random House, 1970), pp. 8–9.

18. See especially Angus Campbell, "The Passive Citizen," *Acta Sociologica,* 6 (1962), 9–12, reprinted in William J. Crotty, Donald M. Freeman, and Douglas S. Gatlin (eds.), *Political Parties and Political Behavior* (Boston: Allyn & Bacon, 1966), pp. 400–414; and William Kornhauser, *The Politics of Mass Society* (Glencoe, Ill.: Free Press, 1959).

19. Hazel Erskine, "The Polls: Corruption in Government," *Public Opinion Quarterly,* 37 (Winter, 1973–1974), 628.

Chapter 5

1. Martha Harris scored a 5 on the composite political alienation index, showing a *disillusioned* but not extremely alienated combination of feelings. Martha is extremely disinterested in politics, expressing lack of concern on all three of the political apathy questions. These answers, combined with her statement that she did not vote in 1972, we call an "indifferent" response.

2. While 45 percent of the apathetic respondents said that they voted in 1972, less than 12 percent said that they attempted to influence the voting choice of others. Apathetic citizens are even less likely to engage in other forms of political participation, such as wearing campaign buttons, attending political meetings, and contributing to a candidate or party.

3. Approximately 56 percent of the respondents gave disillusioned responses in 1972; that is, they scored between 3 and 6 on the composite political alienation scale. Of these disillusioned citizens, more than one-quarter gave politically disinterested responses to the three apathy questions.

4. See Michael Parenti's intriguing comments on "Nonvoting as

a Rational Response," and "Voting as an Irrational Response," *Democracy for the Few* (New York: St. Martin's Press, 1974), pp. 158–165.

5. E. E. Schattschneider, *The Semi-Sovereign People* (New York: Holt, Rinehart and Winston, 1960), p. 104.

6. Seymour Martin Lipset, *Political Man: The Social Bases of Politics* (Garden City, N.Y.: Doubleday, 1963), p. 229. On the point concerning authoritarianism, David Riesman notes that political apathy may be a passive counterforce to complete domination by an authoritarian regime. *Individualism Reconsidered* (Glencoe, Ill.: Free Press, 1954), pp. 414–425.

7. Heinz Eulau, "The Politics of Happiness," *Antioch Review*, 16 (1956), 259–264.

8. See, for example, Schattschneider, *The Semi-Sovereign People*, pp. 103–109. Here, nonvoting is equated to abstention and "boycott of the political system." In Lipset, *Political Man*, pp. 183–229, nonvoting appears to be a working definition of apathy.

9. Apathy and Alienation—1972 (in percentages)

	Allegiance	Disillusion	Alienation
Interest	94	78	56
Apathy	6	22	44
Total	100	100	100

n = 972   Gamma = .59   Chi-square significant at .0001

10. Directors of the ISR surveys have noted:

If we compare the proportions of our samples that reported voting for President (74 percent in 1952, 73 percent in 1956) with the proportion of the civilian population of voting age that voted (63 percent in 1952, 60 percent in 1956) a difference of about 12 percentage points is found. Some of this difference is due to the fact that a few of our respondents have told us they voted when in fact they did not. Yet much more of the difference comes from sources quite unrelated to errors of individual report. Angus Campbell, Philip E. Converse, Warren E. Miller, and Donald E. Stokes, *The American Voter* (New York: Wiley, 1960), p. 94.

Political Alienation

11. Respondents' Attempt to Influence the Vote of Others by Alienation, by Apathy—1972 (in percentages)

Tries to Influence Others' Vote	Interested			Apathetic		
	Allegiance	Disillusion	Alienation	Allegiance	Disillusion	Alienation
Tries	52	44	34	17	13	10
Doesn't Try	48	56	66	83	87	90
Total	100	100	100	100	100	100
	(193)	(425)	(125)	(12)	(117)	(100)

Chi-square significant at .009   Chi-square not significant

12. Respondents' Voting Participation by Alienation, by Apathy—1972 (in percentages)

Voting Participation	Interested			Apathetic		
	Allegiance	Disillusion	Alienation	Allegiance	Disillusion	Alienation
Voted	91	80	69	75	43	44
Did Not Vote	9	20	31	25	57	56
Total	100	100	100	100	100	100
	(193)	(425)	(125)	(12)	(117)	(100)

Chi-square significant at .0001   Chi-square significant at .10

13. Apathetic Americans were seven times as likely to take the view that their vote "wouldn't make any difference" because so many millions of people vote as those who expressed an interest in politics.

14. This would appear to raise a serious objection to Professor Eulau's "politics of happiness" argument, "Politics of Happiness."

15. In the early 1960s Professor Timothy Leary of Harvard University became the leading spokesman for the therapeutic, social, and

religious value of psychedelic drugs and the lysergic acid derivitive known as LSD. In 1962 Leary established a Psychedelic Training Center in Mexico, but this effort was short lived. After numerous troubles with federal and state authorities on drug-related charges, he fled the country but later returned to face trial and subsequent imprisonment. Author Ken Kesey's widely unique "trip" into the drug culture is set down in a fascinating chronicle by Tom Wolfe, *The Electric Kool-Aid Acid Test* (New York: Farrar, Straus & Giroux, 1968).

16. Theodore Roszak, *The Making of a Counter Culture* (Garden City, N.Y.: Doubleday, 1969), pp. 32–40.

17. *Ibid.*, p. 40.

18. Charles Reich, *The Greening of America* (New York: Random House, 1970), p. 4.

19. Malcolm Muggeridge, "Unresisting Imbecility," in Philip Nobile (ed.), *The Con II Controversy* (New York: Pocket Books, 1971), pp. 1–2.

20. Stewart Alsop, "A Bag of Scary Mush," *Newsweek* (November 9, 1970), reprinted in *ibid.*, pp. 2–5.

21. Political Apathy and Interest by Annual Family Income—1972 (in percentages)

Political Interest	Annual Family Income (in $)				
	0-3,999	4,000-5,000	6,000-9,999	10,000-14,999	over 15,000
Interested	66	73	75	79	86
Apathetic	34	27	25	21	14
Total	100	100	100	100	100
	(478)	(292)	(612)	(585)	(537)

Chi-square significant at .001

22. Analysis of the election data has clearly shown that many people in Jenny's situation—low income, poor education, and residence in a ghetto—are also low on interest in politics. Penn Kimball puts the point this way:

Voter participation has always exhibited a high correlation with education and income, two spheres of urban disadvantage. . . .

Tenements, rooming houses, and housing projects—the dormitories of the ghetto electorate—provide, furthermore, a shifting, changing human environment instead of the social reinforcements that encourage political involvement in more stable neighborhoods. And the immediate struggle for subsistence drains the reservoirs of emotional energy available for the distant and complex realm of politics. . . . Elections come and go, and the life of poverty goes on pretty much as before, neither dramatically better nor dramatically worse. The posturing of candidates and the promises of parties are simply irrelevant to the daily grind of marginal existence." *The Disconnected* (New York: Columbia University Press, 1972), pp. 16–17.

23. See Donald E. Stokes, "Popular Evaluations of Government: An Empirical Assessment," in Harlan Cleveland and Harold D. Lasswell (eds.), *Ethics and Bigness* (New York: Harper & Row, 1962).

Chapter 6

1. *Time* (December 17, 1973), p. 33.
2. Fortunately, the sheer terror of an abrupt and heated end to cold war confrontations was muted by the voluminous verbiage of megatons, second-strike capabilities, flexible response, and so forth. As Harold Rosenberg once observed, "America masks its terrors behind patterns of fact." *The Tradition of the New* (New York: Horizon Press, 1959), p. 269.
3. In its 1964 presidential election survey, The Institute for Social Research had not yet begun to include questions to measure approval of various protest tactics. Such questions first appeared in the 1968 survey.
4. On April 24, 1971, an antiwar rally was held on the grounds of the Capitol with a crowd variously estimated at from 200,000 to 500,000 people, the largest number ever to attend a single demonstration in Washington. The following week the "Mayday Tribe" attempted to disrupt Washington traffic. Operating under a set of questionable guidelines established by Attorney General John Mitchell, Washington police arrested an estimated 7,000 persons.

5. Respondents' Opinion of Trade with Communist Countries by Alienation—1972 (in percentages)

Government Allowance of Trade	Allegiance	Disillusion	Alienation
Should Allow	76	66	50
Should *Not* Allow	24	34	50
Total	100	100	100
	(168)	(400)	(133)

6. Respondents' Opinion of Aid to Countries Different from the United States by Alienation—1972 (in percentages)

Opinion of Foreign Aid	Allegiance	Disillusion	Alienation
Approve	57	48	39
Disapprove	43	52	61
Total	100	100	100
	(199)	(527)	(216)

7. Like many white working men, Aaron Rouse is a proud veteran who "put in my time" with the military. Aaron saw action in Korea, and he witnessed a number of his buddies lose their lives during the long winter of 1952. Quite often such men are first or second generation Americans who have little time for military half measures and "draft dodgers" and who make a considerable show of their patriotism. As columnist Pete Hamill describes it:

> Patriotism is very important to the working-class white man. Most of the time he is the son of an immigrant, and most immigrants sincerely believe that the Pledge of Allegiance, the Star Spangled Banner, the American flag are symbols of what it means to be Americans. . . . On "I am an American" Day they march in parades with a kind of religious fervor that can look absurd to the outsider. . . . Walk through any working-class white neighborhood and you will see dozens of veterans' clubs, named after neighborhood men who were killed in World War II or Korea. . . . they are places where an odd sort of know-nothingism is fostered. "The Revolt of the White Lower Middle Class," in Louise Kapp Howe (ed.), *The White Majority* (New York: Vintage, 1970), p. 17.

8. Respondents' Opinions on Dealing with Urban Unrest by Alienation—1972 (seven-point scale in percentages)

Opinion on Seven-Point Scale	Allegiance	Disillusion	Alienation
Solve Urban Problems (#1)	28	35	41
Mixed or Moderate Response (#2-6)	64	51	44
Use all Available Force (#7)	8	14	15
Total	100	100	100
	(190)	(498)	(188)

9. Theodore H. White, *The Making of the President: 1968* (New York: Atheneum, 1969), p. 431. Multidimensional analysis conducted by the authors of the 1968 national presidential election survey taken before Robert Kennedy was assassinated shows that the shift of Kennedy's support to Wallace was very likely to have been as real as it was apparent. Kennedy and Wallace supporters shared a number of the same social and economic characteristics.

10. In the final count, Governor Wallace won 9,906,141 votes or 13.53 percent of the total vote of 73,186,819.

11. Apropos of the position of blacks during the civil rights movement, E. E. Schattschneider has pointed out that

it is the weak, not the strong, who appeal to public authority for relief. It is the weak who want to socialize conflict, i.e., to involve more and more people in the conflict until the balance of forces is changed. In the school yard it is not the bully, but the defenseless smaller boys who "tell the teacher." When the teacher intervenes the balance of power in the school yard is apt to change drastically. It is the function of public authority to *modify private power relations by enlarging the scope of the conflict. The Semi-Sovereign People* (New York: Holt, Rinehart and Winston, 1960), p. 40.

Accordingly, it was southern whites in prevailing local power structures who complained of "outside agitators" enlarging the scope of local conflict and charged that the federal government (i.e., "the teacher") was interfering with the "sovereign rights" of the states.

12. An excellent case study of this series of incidents has been written by Corinne Silverman, *The Little Rock Story,* Inter-University Case Program #41, rev. ed. (Indianapolis: Bobbs-Merrill, 1959); see also Richard E. Neustadt, *Presidential Power* (New York: Wiley, 1960), pp. 16–32.

13. Thoughtful accounts of the civil rights movement include Kenneth B. Clark, *The Negro Protest* (Boston: Beacon Press, 1963); Louis Lomax, *The Negro Revolt* (New York: Harper & Row, 1962); and Charles E. Silberman, *Crisis in Black and White* (New York: Random House, 1964).

14. A year-by-year account of this development, from a "movement" viewpoint, is found in Mitchell Goodman (ed.), *The Movement Toward a New America* (New York: Knopf, 1970).

15. Between December 31, 1964, and December 31, 1965, U.S. armed forces in South Vietnam (not including peripheral island bases) increased from 23,300 to 184,300. During 1964 some 147 Americans were killed in action. In 1965 the number killed jumped to 1,369, and 6,114 were wounded. U.S. Department of Defense figures, January 22, 1969, quoted in *Congress and the Nation* (Washington, D.C.: Congressional Quarterly Service, 1969), vol. 2, p. 53.

16. *Ibid.*

17. A literate and moving account of the demonstration is found in Norman Mailer, *The Armies of the Night* (New York: New American Library, 1968).

18. For an excellent treatment of the stages of developing conflict behavior, see James S. Coleman, *Community Conflict* (Gencoe, Ill.: Free Press, 1957). A more complete typology and theoretical treatment of conflicts is located in Neil J. Smelser, *Theory of Collective Behavior* (New York: Free Press, 1962).

19. See especially *Report of the National Advisory Commission on Civil Disorders* (Washington, D.C.: U.S. Government Printing Office, 1968); Stanley Lieberson and Arnold R. Silverman, "The Precipitants and Underlying Conditions of Race Riots," *American Sociological Review,* 30 (December 1965), 887–898; and Robert M. Fogelson, "Violence as Protest," in Robert H. Connery (ed.), *Urban Riots: Violence and Social Change* (New York: Proceedings of the Academy of Political Science, Columbia University, 1968), vol. 19, pp. 25–41.

20. See David Brustien, "News Theater," *New York Times Magazine,* June 16, 1974.

21. U.S. Immigration and Naturalization Service, Department of Justice, *Annual Report* (Washington, D.C.: Government Printing Office, 1950, 1968, 1973).

22. *New York Times* (September 28, 1972).

23. *New York Times* (September 25, 1974).

24. *Ibid.*

25. *New York Post* (September 16, 1974).

26. Lewis Coser, *The Functions of Social Conflict* (Glencoe, Ill.: Free Press, 1956), pp. 37–38. Coser has defined *legitimacy* as "a crucial intervening variable without which it is impossible to predict whether feelings of hostility arising out of an unequal distribution of privileges and rights will actually lead to conflict." *Ibid.*, p. 37.

27. *Mora* v. *McNamara*, 389 US 934 (1967).

28. See James A. Michener, *Kent State* (New York: Random House, 1971).

29. David Easton, *A Systems Analysis of Political Life* (New York: Wiley, 1965), p. 282. Other useful sources on the problem of legitimacy include Talcott Parsons, *The Social System* (Glencoe, Ill.: Free Press, 1951), and S. N. Eisenstadt, *The Political Systems of Empires* (New York: Free Press, 1963).

Chapter 7

1. U.S. Senate, Testimony by Louis Harris, President, Louis Harris and Associates, 93rd Cong., 1st Sess., December 3, 1973, *Congressional Record*, S.21704.

2. *Ibid.*, S.21705.

3. Primary theoretical and empirical sources include Talcott Parsons, *The Social System* (Glencoe, Ill.: Free Press, 1951); Talcott Parsons and R. F. Bales, *Family Socialization and Interaction Process* (Glencoe, Ill.: Free Press, 1955); Myron J. Levy, Jr., *The Structure of Society* (Princeton, N.J.: Princeton University Press, 1952); and Herbert Hyman, *Political Socialization* (Glencoe, Ill.: Free Press, 1959).

4. See especially David Easton, *A Framework for Political Analysis* (Englewood Cliffs, N.J.: Prentice-Hall, 1965), and *A Systems Analysis of Political Life* (New York: Wiley, 1965).

5. David Easton and Jack Dennis, *Children in the Political System: Origins of Political Legitimacy* (New York: McGraw-Hill, 1969).

6. *Ibid.*, p. 287.

7. See Fred I. Greenstein, *Children and Politics* (New Haven, Conn.: Yale University Press, 1965); "Popular Images of the Presi-

dent," *American Journal of Psychiatry,* 122 (November 1965), 523–29; Robert D. Hess and Judith Torney, *The Development of Political Attitudes in Children* (Chicago: University of Chicago Press, 1967); and Roberta Siegel, "Image of a President: Some Insights into the Political View of School Children," *American Political Science Review,* 62 (March 1968), 216–226. Easton and Dennis, in their study of children's political views involving over 12,000 interviews, "were unable to find a child who did not express highest esteem for the President." *Children in the Political System,* p. 177. In Dean Jaros' study of children's political attitudes in the mid-1960s, he found that black children respond to the President in positive terms similar to those of white children. "Children's Orientations Towards the President: Some Additional Theoretical Considerations and Data," *Journal of Politics,* 29 (1967), 368–387.

8. F. Christopher Arterton, "The Impact of Watergate on Children's Attitudes Toward Political Authority," *Political Science Quarterly,* 89 (June 1974), 274. "By margins of two-to-one in the third grade, two-and-a-half-to-one in the fourth, and three-to-one in the fifth grade, today's children believe that the president should be impeached [in 1973]. These are remarkable figures given the fact that these children's parents voted two-to-one for Nixon only a year earlier." *Ibid.,* p. 283. See also Robert P. Hawkins, Suzanne P. Hawkins, and Donald F. Roberts, "Political Socialization of Children: Two Studies of Responses to Watergate" in Sidney Kraus (ed.), *Watergate and Mass Communications,* (Bloomington, Ind.: University of Indiana Press, forthcoming).

9. *Ibid.,* p. 278.

10. *Ibid.,* p. 285.

11. The very first of the major empirically based national election studies learned immediately the facts of family political solidarity: "Among husbands and wives, both of whom had decided to vote, only one pair in 22 disagreed. Among parents and children, one pair in 12 disagreed. . . ." Paul F. Lazarsfeld, *et al., The People's Choice* (New York: Columbia University Press, 1944), p. 141. These findings have been reinforced by every study since.

12. Easton and Dennis, *Children in the Political System,* p. 290.

13. Arterton, "The Impact of Watergate," p. 288.

14. This assessment probably represents the typical summary judgment of the latter-day pluralist; not to say that everyone, or even a majority, takes this view. The battle of "elitist" and "pluralist" interpretations of American politics has raged for many years in the

voluminous and ever expanding professional literature of political scientists and sociologists. Among the best extended arguments in this debate are C. Wright Mills, *The Power Elite* (New York: Oxford University Press, 1956); G. William Domhoff, *Who Rules America?* (Englewood Cliffs, N.J.: Prentice-Hall, 1967); Robert A. Dahl, *Who Governs?* (New Haven, Conn.: Yale University Press, 1961); and Nelson W. Polsby, *Community Power and Political Theory* (New Haven, Conn.: Yale University Press, 1963.)

15. The italics represent underlinings in the candidate's own text. Quoted in Theodore H. White, *The Making of the President: 1964* (New York: Atheneum, 1965), p. 217.

16. The "manifest and latent functions" of the political party machine, most maligned of American political institutions, are superbly analyzed in Robert K. Merton, *Social Theory and Social Structure* (Glencoe, Ill.: Free Press, 1957), pp. 70–81.

17. Theodore Kheel was a widely successful labor arbitrator and federal mediator during the 1960s and early 1970s.

18. Robert L. Heilbroner, *An Inquiry into the Human Prospect* (New York: Norton, 1974), pp. 42–43.

19. Adolf A. Berle, Jr., and Gardner C. Means, *The Modern Corporation and Private Property* (New York: Macmillan, 1932). See also A. D. H. Kaplan, *Big Business in a Competitive System* (Washington, D.C.: Brookings Institution, 1954); and Norman R. Collins and Lee E. Preston, "The Size Structure of the Largest Industrial Firms, 1909–1958," *American Economic Review,* 51, no. 5 (February 1961), 986–1011. Collins and Preston conclude:

> The clearest long-run trends in the shape and stability of the size structure of the industrial giants during this half-century are: (1) a decline in the frequency of change in the identities of the giant firms, (2) a decline in the frequency of change in relative size positions among the giants, and (3) a slight tendency for the giant firms to become more nearly equal in relative size. . . . there is *considerable* reason to believe that firms now at the top of the industrial pyramid *are* more likely to remain there than were their predecessors. *Ibid.,* p. 1001.

20. John Kenneth Galbraith, *The New Industrial State* (Boston: Houghton Mifflin, 1967), pp. 1–2.

21. Heilbroner explains that prices are often "set by leading firms, rather than by the interplay of competition among many firms. . . ." The fact that prices are *administered* "does not mean that in each of

these industries firms do not vie with one another. On the contrary, if you ask a General Motors or a U.S. Steel executive, he will tell you that Ford had edged out General Motors in such-and-such a line, or that Bethlehem Steel has captured some of U.S. Steel's business. The point, however, is *that the competition among oligopolists typically utilizes every means except one: price cutting."* Robert L. Heilbroner, *The Making of Economic Society* (Englewood Cliffs, N.J.: Prentice-Hall, 1962), pp. 133–134.

22. Galbraith, *The New Industrial State*, p. 296.

23. Heilbroner, *The Making of Economic Society*, p. 165.

24. After returning from this conference, economist Milton Friedman wrote:

Labor. This was a large group. It was prominently represented on the podium. . . .

The people who spoke from the podium and the labor members of the [White House Labor-Management] committee are all officials of labor *unions.* Yet only about one-fourth of all U.S. workers are members of labor unions. . . .

Labor-union officials would no doubt claim that all workers have common interests and that in speaking for union members they are speaking for all workers. . . . [But] the unionized sector is in conflict with the non-unionized sector. High wages obtained by any one union mean fewer jobs in the trade involved, hence more competition and lower wages for other jobs. Higher wages for union members as a whole mean lower wages for non-unionized workers. "Who Represents Whom? *Newsweek* (October 14, 1974), p. 104.

25. Richard N. Goodwin, *The American Condition* (New York: Doubleday, 1974), p. 225.

26. *Ibid.,* p. 285.

27. See J. Leiper Freeman, *The Political Process: Executive Bureau-Legislative Committee Relations,* rev. ed. (New York: Random House, 1965); Douglass Cater, *Power in Washington* (New York: Random House, 1964); Galbraith, *The New Industrial State,* pp. 296–317.

28. Heilbroner, *An Inquiry into the Human Prospect,* p. 84.

29. John Kenneth Galbraith, *Economics and the Public Purpose* (Boston: Houghton Mifflin, 1973), p. 100.

30. Heilbroner, *An Inquiry into the Human Prospect,* p. 14.

31. *Bulletin of the Atomic Scientists* (July 1974), p. 30.

32. Rachel Carson, *Silent Spring* (Boston: Houghton Mifflin, 1962).

33. Excellent sources on environmental hazards and the political movement associated with environmental and conservation problems include Barry Commoner, *The Closing Circle* (New York: Knopf, 1971); Paul and Ann Ehrlich, *Population, Resources, Environment* (San Francisco: Freeman, 1972); Frank Graham, Jr., *Since Silent Spring* (Boston: Houghton Mifflin, 1970); Walter A. Rosenbaum, *The Politics of Environmental Concern* (New York: Praeger, 1973); and Stewart L. Udall, *The Quiet Crisis* (New York: Holt, Rinehart, and Winston, 1963).

34. Donella H. Meadows, *et al., The Limits to Growth: A Report for the Club of Rome's Project on the Predicament of Mankind* (New York: Universe Books, 1972).

35. Paraphrased by James Reston, "Waiting for Jerry," *New York Times* (October 2, 1974).

36. During October 1974 President Ford launched a publicity campaign against inflation, issuing 100,000 "WIN" (Whip Inflation Now) buttons.

37. Michael Tanzer, *The Sick Society: An Economic Examination* (New York: Holt, Rinehart and Winston, 1971), pp. 188–209.

38. Hillel Black, *Buy Now, Pay Later* (New York: Morrow, 1961).

39. "Years of Excessive Credit Expansion," *New York Times* (October 27, 1974).

40. See Robert Triffin, *Gold and the Dollar Crisis* (New Haven, Conn.: Yale University Press, 1961); Tanzer, *The Sick Society,* pp. 167–187; and Charles F. Stewart, "Energy and the Balance of Payments," in Robert H. Connery and Robert S. Gilmour (eds.), *The National Energy Problem* (Lexington, Mass.: Lexington Books, 1974).

41. William D. Smith, "Oil Upsets the Balance of Power," *New York Times* (September 29, 1974).

42. *New York Times* (June 30, 1974).

43. See William E. Leuchtenburg, *Franklin D. Roosevelt and the New Deal* (New York: Harper & Row, 1963), pp. 13–16.

44. The American response to the Depression is nowhere better illustrated than in Studs Terkel's superb oral history *Hard Times* (New York: Avon Books, 1970).

45. Eric Hoffer, "What We Have Lost," *New York Times Magazine* (October 20, 1974), p. 114.

46. Paul Starr, "Rebels After the Cause: Living with Contradictions, *New York Times Magazine* (October 13, 1974), p. 100.

Index

Aberbach, Joel, 169n
Ackerman, Nathan, 176n
Action, political, *see* Political action
Affluence, allegiance, age, and, 74-78
Age, alienation and, 63-65; allegiance, affluence, and, 74-78; *see also* Elderly, the; Youth
Agger, Robert E., 169n, 174n, 176n, 178n
Agnew, Spiro T., 3
Aiken, Michael, 175n
Alienation, political, 3-21; definitions of, 5-11; examples of, 1-3; measurement of, 11-21; origins of idea of, 6-11, 166, 167; *see also specific topics*
Allegiance, decline of, 69-91; political participation and, 80-84, 179n
Almond, Gabriel, 169n, 173n, 178n
Alsop, Stewart, 105, 183n
American Civil Liberties Union, 102
American Independent Party, 124, 125
American Revolution, 71
Amundsen, Kirsten, 175n
Anarchists, 10
Anomie, 88, 179n
Antiwar movement, 128-31, 134, 184n; *see also* Student movement
Apathy, political, 20, 92-111; abstainers and, 107-9; definition of, 95; income and, 106, 183n;

nature of, 94-98; participation and, 180n; reformers and, 109-10; scale of, 95-96, 164-65; withdrawal and, 103-7, 182n
Apter, David, E., 168n
Aptheker, Herbert, 167n
Arabs, 154
Arterton, F. Christopher, 145, 189n
Arthur, Alan, 59, 61-63, 107-9
Arthur, Jean, 61-63, 107-9
Avineri, Shlomo, 167n
Avorn, Jerry L., 176n
Axelson, L. J., 176n

Baczko, B., 166n
Bales, R. F., 188n
Bell, Daniel, 168n
Beloit, Ward, 33, 35-37
Benson, Oliver, 163n
Bent, Dale H., 160n
Berelson, Bernard R., 178n
Berger, Peter L. and Brigitte, 176n
Berle, A. A., 149, 190n
Berrigan, Daniel and Philip, 46, 174n
Binzen, Peter, 172n
Birnbaum, Eugene A., 155
Black, Hillel, 192n
Black people, 16-18, 24, 26, 170-72n
Blanner, Robert, 173n
Bottomore, T. B., 167n
Brown, H. Rap, 118
Brustien, David, 187n
Budeau, Jack, 65-67
Bullough, Bonnie, 172n

193

Index

Campbell, Angus, 169n, 179n, 180n, 181n
Cambodia, 41, 102
Cantril, Hadley, 179n
Carson, Rachael, 153, 191n
Casey, William VanEtten, 174n
Cater, Douglass, 191n
Cayton, Horace R., 171n
Chalmers, David M., 173n
Chappaquiddick incident, 15
Children, socialization of, 143-46
Christian thought, 6
Citizenship, renunciation of, 132-34
Civil Rights Act, 130
Civil Rights Commission, New York State, 51
Civil rights movement, 126-28, 130, 131, 187n
Clark, Kenneth B., 187n
Cleveland, Harlan, 184n
Club of Rome, 154
Cold war, 40, 120
Coleman, James S., 187n
Collins, Norman R., 190n
Commercialism, 8
Committee to Impeach the President, 46
Commoner, Barry, 192n
Communism, 120, 123
Congress of Racial Equality, 23
Connery, Robert H., 187n, 192n
Conservatism, 71
Constitution, U.S., 4
Converse, Philip E., 169n, 179n, 181n
Coser, Lewis, 134, 188n
Crotty, William J., 180n
Cuban missile crisis, 115

Dahl, Robert A., 190n
Dean, Dwight, 168n
Democratic Party (Democrats), 4, 33, 37, 46, 83, 107, 109, 125, 157-59, 170-71n, 179n; black people and, 16-18, 170n; 1968 convention of, 41, 52, 124, 130; see also Independent Democrats
Dennis, Jack, 144-46, 188n, 189n
Dentler, Robert A., 170n
Desegregation, 22
Dewey, Thomas, 62

Disillusionment, political, 18, 19, 141-43; defined, 5
Dissent, milieu of, 113-15; see also Protest movements
Distrust, sense of, 3-5, 13-14, 16; indicators of, 160-61, 163
Dixiecrat movement, 179n
Domhoff, G. William, 190n
Draft evaders, 132, 133
Drake, St. Clair, 171n
Dryden, Arnold, 78-80
Dubey, S. N., 172n
Durkheim, Émile, 168n, 179n

Eagleton, Thomas, 20
Easton, David, 140, 144-46, 188n, 189n
Economic basis of alienation, 149-52, 154-55
Economy, prospects for the, 152-59
Education, alienation and, 46-48; for women, 55
Ehrlich, Paul and Ann, 192n
Eisenhower, Dwight D., 62, 127, 170n
Eisenstadt, S. N., 188n
Elderly, the, 67-68; see also Age
Epstein, Cynthia Fuchs, 175n
Erbe, William, 174n, 178n
Erskine, Hazel, 180n
Eulau, Heinz, 95, 181n, 182n
Evers, Medgar, 115, 128
Extremism, see Polarization, political

Fairfield, Richard, 168n
Farm Bureau Federation, 36
Faubus, Orval, 127
Fendrich, J. A., 176n
Feuer, Lewis, 166n, 167n, 168n
Finifter, Ada W., 10, 169n
Fogelson, Robert M., 187n
Ford, Gerald, 2, 18, 150, 156, 192n
Franklin, Ben A., 173n
Free, Lloyd A., 179n
Freedom rides, 127
Freeman, Donald M., 180n
Freeman, J. Leiper, 191n
Friedman, Milton, 191n
Friedman, Robert, 176n

194

195

Index

196

Index

198